CONTENTS

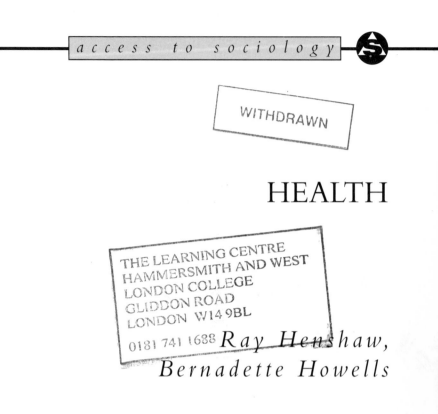

access to sociology

WITHDRAWN

HEALTH

Ray Henshaw,
Bernadette Howells

Series Editor: Paul Selfe

Hodder & Stoughton
A MEMBER OF THE HODDER HEADLINE GROUP

ACKNOWLEDGEMENTS

We would like to thank all of our friends and family whose interest and support sustained us when we were writing this book. Many thanks to Llinos Edwards for suggesting that we write the book and to Paul Selfe for the advice and assistance. Thanks also to Emma Knights for her patience over choosing the cover image and to Pat Stevens for the typing support. We would like to thank Age Concern for their help in resourcing the health problems faced by the elderly.

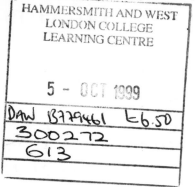
Orders: please contact Bookpoint Ltd, 39 Milton Park, Abingdon, Oxon OX14 4TD. Telephone: (44) 01235 400414, Fax: (44) 01235 400454. Lines are open from 9.00–6.00, Monday to Saturday, with a 24 hour message answering service. Email address: orders@bookpoint.co.uk

A catalogue record for this title is available from The British Library

ISBN 0 340 74286 0

First published 1999
Impression number 10 9 8 7 6 5 4 3 2 1
Year   2005 2004 2003 2002 2001 2000 1999

Cover photo of Louis Pasteur in his laboratory, Albert Edelfelt; The Bridgeman Art Library

Typeset by Transet Limited, Coventry, England.
Printed in Great Britain for Hodder & Stoughton Educational, a division of Hodder Headline plc, 338 Euston Road, London NW1 3BH by Redwood Books, Trowbridge, Wilts.

1

INTRODUCTION

HOW TO USE THE BOOK

EACH CHAPTER IN this book examines one or more of the central debates relating to the sociology of media. The text is devised for readers with little or no background knowledge in the subject, and there are Study Points and Activities throughout to encourage a consideration of the issues raised. Student readers are advised to make use of these and answer them either on paper or in group discussion, a particularly fruitful way of learning; they will assist them to develop the skills of interpretation, analysis and evaluation. There are many ways of preparing for an exam, but a thorough understanding of the material is obviously crucial.

Each chapter is structured to give a clear understanding of the authors, concepts and issues that you need to know about. To assist understanding and facilitate later revision, it is often helpful to make concise notes.

MAKING NOTES FROM THE BOOK

Linear notes
- Bold headings establish key points: names, theories and concepts.
- Subheadings indicate details of relevant issues.
- A few numbered points list related arguments.

Diagram or pattern notes
- Use a large blank sheet of paper and write a key idea in the centre.
- Make links between this and related issues.
- Show also the connections between sub issues which share features in common.

Both systems have their advantages and disadvantages, and may take some time to perfect. Linear notes can be little more than a copy of what is already in the book and patterned notes can be confusing. But if you practise the skill, they can reduce material efficiently and concisely becoming invaluable for revision. Diagrammatic notes may be very useful for those with a strong visual memory and provide a clear overview of a whole issue, showing patterns of interconnection. The introduction of helpful drawings or a touch of humour into the format is often a good way to facilitate the recall of names, research studies and complex concepts.

Activity

- Make a diagram to show the two ways of making notes with their possible advantages and disadvantages

SKILLS ADVICE

Students must develop and display certain skills for their examination and recognise which ones are being tested in a question. The clues are frequently in key words in the opening part. The skill domains are:

1 **Knowledge and understanding:** the ability to discuss the views of the main theorists; their similarities and differences; the strengths and weaknesses of evidence. To gain marks students must display this when asked to *explain, examine, suggest a method, outline reasons.*
2 **Interpretation, application and analysis:** the use of evidence in a logical, relevant way, either to show how it supports arguments or refutes them. Students must show this ability when asked *identify, use items A/B/C, draw conclusions from a table.*
3 **Evaluation:** the skill of assessing evidence in a balanced way so that logical conclusions follow. Students can recognise this skill when asked to *assess, critically examine, comment on levels of reliability, compare and contrast,* or if asked *to what extent.*

Activity

Draw an evaluation table, as below, using the whole of an A4 page. Examine studies as you proceed in your work and fill in the relevant details. Keep it for revision purposes.

Sociologist		
Title of the study	Strengths	Weaknesses
Verdict		
Judgement/justification		

REVISION ADVICE

- Keep clear notes at all times in a file or on disk (with back up copy).
- Be familiar with exam papers and their demands.
- Become familiar with key authors, their theories, their research and sociological concepts.

Activity

Make and keep **Key Concept Cards**, as shown below.

COLLECTIVE CONSCIENCE

Key idea

A term used by **Durkheim** meaning:

- The existence of a social and moral order exterior to individuals and acting upon them as an independent force.
- The shared sentiments, beliefs and values of individuals which make up the **collective conscience.**
- In **traditional societies** it forms the basis of social order.
- As societies modernise the collective conscience weakens: **mechanical solidarity** is replaced by **organic solidarity**.

Key theorist: Emile Durkheim

Syllabus area: Functionalism

EXAMINATION ADVICE

To develop an effective method of writing, answers should be:

- **Sociological:** use the language and research findings of sociologists; do not use anecdotal opinion gathered from people not involved in sociology to support arguments.

- **Adequate in length:** enough is written to obtain the marks available.
- **Interconnected** with other parts of the syllabus (such as stratification, gender, ethnicity).
- **Logical:** the answer follows from the relevant evidence.
- **Balanced:** arguments and counter arguments are weighed; references are suitable.
- **Accurate:** reliable data is obtained from many sources.

The three skill areas on p 2 should be demonstrated, so that the question is answered effectively.

In displaying knowledge, the student is not necessarily also demonstrating interpretation.

- This must be specified with phrases like 'Therefore, this study leads to the view that...'
- Sections of answers should hang together, one leading to the next. This shows how the question is being answered by a process of analysis based on the evidence.
- Reach a conclusion based on the evidence used and the interpretations made.

The skill of evaluation is often regarded (not necessarily accurately) as the most problematic. Evaluation means being judge and jury; the strengths and weaknesses of evidence is assessed and an overall judgement about its value is made. To evaluate an argument or theory, consider whether it usefully opens up debate; explains the events studied; does it have major weaknesses?

Activity

Look through some past examination papers and pick out the evaluation questions. Underline the evaluation words and work out which skills are required.

COURSEWORK ADVICE

Coursework provides an opportunity to carry out a study using primary and/or secondary data to investigate an issue of sociological interest, and must address theoretical issues. The suggestions included at the end of each chapter may be adapted or used to generate further ideas. Final decision must be agreed with a teacher or tutor.

MAKING A PLAN

Before starting a piece of coursework, you should make a plan:

1 Read and make notes from articles describing research projects in journals.
2 Have a clear aim in mind; choose an issue that interests you and is within your ability.
3 Decide more precisely what you want to know; establish a simple hypothesis to test.
4 Select a range of possible methods; consider both quantitative and qualitative.
5 Decide on a range of possible sources of information.
6 List the people to whom you can seek help, perhaps including a statistician.

WRITING THE PROJECT

1 Seek frequent advice from a teacher or tutor.
2 Check the weighting for different objectives in the marking scheme.
3 Keep clear notes throughout, including new ideas and any problems that arise.
4 Limit its length (maximum 5,000 words).
5 Label and index the study in the following way:
    a **Rationale:** a reason for choosing the subject; preliminary observations on the chosen area
    b **Context:** an outline of the theoretical and empirical context of the study
    c **Methodology:** a statement of the methodology used and reasons for selecting it
    d **Content:** presentation of the evidence and/or argument including results
    e **Evaluation:** the outcomes are weighed and strengths and weaknesses noted.
    f **Sources:** all the sources of information are listed.
OR
    a **Title**
    b **Contents**
    c **Abstract:** a brief summary of the aims, methods, findings and evaluation.
    d **Rationale**
    e **The Study**
    f **Research Diary**
    g **Bibliography**
    h **Appendix:** to include proposal for the study, single examples of a questionnaire or other data-gathering instrument and transcripts of interviews.
    i **Annex:** to include raw data gathered.

Paul Selfe
Series editor

2

DEFINING HEALTH

Introduction

THE SOCIOLOGY OF health and illness is one of the fastest growing areas within sociology – both in terms of research and teaching.

Sociology cannot claim to explain the whole phenomena of health and illness. However, it offers insights which, in themselves, can be quite profound. What gives rise to disease, the social conditions that foster the communication of disease, the remedies offered, the recruitment and training of personnel, and funding of Health Services are all topics within the field of sociology. Of course, broken limbs, infections, and congenital abnormalities are entirely biological, although they have sociological implications in the way in which they are treated, the attitudes of the rest of society to sufferers, and the development of the individuals own self-identify.

Most health professionals study sociology as an important part of their training. This is true whether they are doctors, nurses, physiotherapists, speech therapists – whatever. Health, as an option, is offered on most 'A' Level and Degree courses in sociology and is an integral part of GNVQ Health and Social Care courses. This chapter will explain the sociological setting for the study of health and illness.

The key issues that will be explored in this chapter will focus on three themes:

- The social constructions of health.
- The theoretical explanations of variations within the between societies.
- The measurement of health and illness.

Table 1: *Theorists, concepts and issues in this chapter*			
KEY THEORIST(S)	THEORY	KEY CONCEPTS	KEY ISSUES
Engel	Bio-medical	Illness is physiological and is caused by bio-genetic malfunctioning or infection	• Ill health can only be treated by the appropriate medical professional
Berger and Luckmann	Interactionism	Social construction of illness	• Mortality and illness varies by social class in ways not explained by biological terms alone
World Health Organisation (WHO)	Relativism	Health is not merely the absence of disease	• Ill health occurs when we fall short of complete well-being
McKeown	Interactionism	Improvements in health were occurring before improvements in medical care	• Improvements in sanitation, diet and hygiene were responsible for improved health in the nineteenth and twentieth centuries
Foucault	Post-structuralist	It is impossible to have objective truths and real facts about anything including biological conditions	• Medical discourse empowers medical practitioners and those who benefits from such a way of knowing about the world

THE SOCIAL CONSTRUCTION OF HEALTH

For us to understand the concepts of health and illness as they exist today, it is necessary to understand how they have been viewed historically. Perhaps with this greater knowledge we will not view health and illness as static concepts, but as ones that change in relation to the environments and cultures we live in. A sociological insight to health care may assist us to adapt to and provide for the future health needs of individuals and groups in society.

THE BIO-MEDICAL MODEL AND ITS CRITICS

Traditionally, the study of health and illness has been dominated by the biological sciences. This is not surprising if we view the rise of medicine in the West alongside the rise of science generally during the nineteenth and twentieth centuries. There has been a 'march of progress' from magical and/or religious explanations and cures towards scientific ones. Thus, the growth in complex medical technology and the accompanying development of a medical profession has, as Ivan **Illich** (1975) has pointed out, created societies dependant on these experts and their technologies. Illich argues that this technology, instead of liberating the unwell by providing cures, impoverishes the individual. He argues that treatment-caused disease (**iatrogenic** disease) has caused more suffering than traffic and industrial accidents combined. Far from providing cure-alls, according to Illich, medical science has made illness, pain and death into technical problems instead of personal challenges. Therefore, human self-sufficiency is removed.

Diametrically opposed to Illich's views are those of modern medicine which sees illness as having its origins in the physical. Therefore, *diagnosis* and *cure* are major features of modern health care systems. We have come to accept hospitals, laboratories, clinics etc and the development of health bodies with their own codes of ethics and social powers.

Activity

See if you can chart the history of a medical institution near you. Find out where the first clinic or hospital was – who built it and why? What does this information tell you about health care in those times?

POINTS OF EVALUATION

1   The model of health described above has been called the **bio-medical model** by **Ross Hume Hall** and was heavily criticised by the first sociologists studying health. Hall and others believed that health care systems should be concerned with the 'whole person' (Hall, 1990) and should not be purely concerned with the body as a machine.
2   In the past 25 years sociological analysis has been particularly concerned with questioning the assumptions behind the bio-medical model.
3   It has been pointed out that health and illness are strongly influenced by aspects of social structure. Social factors not only affect life expectancy but also the life chances of individuals, including their chances of contracting diseases and the subsequent nature of the health care they receive.
4   The biomedical model is dominant in Western societies and is a **mechanistic** approach to health. Doctors' concerns have been with treating symptoms – ill health is seen as an objective fact and health as the absence of disease.
5   This view, according to **Engel** (1997) involves 'the notion of the body as a machine, disease as a consequence of breakdown of the machine, and the doctor's task as repair of the machine'.

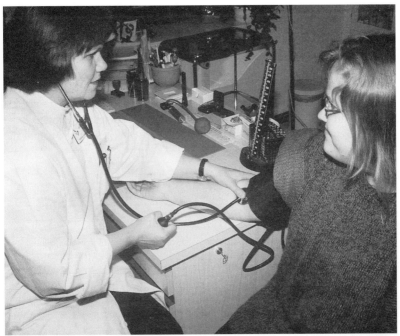

DOCTORS HAVE BEEN ACCUSED OF TAKING A MECHANISTIC APPROACH TO HEALTH, TREATING ONLY THE SYMPTOMS OF ILLNESS, NOT THE WHOLE PERSON.

Ill health has always been a social construct – in early times ill health such as the epilepsy suffered by the Caesars was seen as being 'touched by the Gods'. In medieval times, ill health was seen as a punishment or a 'mark of the devil' (and we have vestiges of this today in the sometimes moralistic treatment of Aids victims or lung cancer victims who are smokers). In more recent or 'modern' times, ill health is more likely to be viewed as purely biological. This can lead to people who feel unwell but who do not fit a sick 'label' being disregarded by society. This will be discussed in Chapter 7. In our post-modern future, ill health may be seen as an intricate mixture of the *psychological, medical, social and environmental.*

What we can say is that, up until modernity, there was always a **Shaman** figure – a holy man who was also a healer. He was the spiritual leader and 'body' doctor combined. In modern society, science came between the two roles and we now have a separation of doctor and spiritual leader. However, the term 'health' can apply to both roles. We may visit the doctor for, say, depression and be given counselling and pills. In the past we would have sought the counsel of a spiritual leader to help us cope or confront the depression.

FOUCAULT

Health care has also been a socially *practical* construction, as suggested by **Michel Foucault**. For example, he argues that it was only the appearance of the clinic that made medical discourse possible. We now live in a world where we take for granted medical concepts and their use in all areas of social life – we even talk about 'healthy' businesses. According to Foucault, when we no longer needed buildings for paupers and madmen – such as workhouses and Bedlam's – these buildings were used increasingly as hospitals and clinics, simply because the buildings were available.

Study point

Carry out research into the definitions of epistemology and ontology. How do these terms help us to understand different interpretations of 'illness'?

ORIGINS OF THE SOCIOLOGY OF HEALTH

The term 'social construction' comes from the work of two interactionist sociologists, **Berger** and **Luckmann** (1966). Their interpretive argument is that both our everyday concepts and the so-called 'taken for granted' features of our world are created through social interaction. They argued that sociology should not judge the different systems of knowledge in different societies, but that it should focus on describing and explaining the social processes involved in their various constructions. They noted that mortality and illness varied by social class and that this could not be explained in biological terms alone. Thus, the very concepts of health and illness vary both cross-culturally and historically. At various times in our history (and indeed in some cultures today) more than ample physical proportions have been viewed positively as healthy and attractive. Today, in the West, at least, slimness is the health goal of both men and women. When we look at mental health social construction can be seen particularly clearly:

- 'Drapetomania' was a mental abnormality black slaves were said to have if they attempted to run away from their natural masters, their white owners.
- Victorian women who admitted to enjoying sex were seen as mad or bad.
- Russian dissidents in Stanlinist Russia were sent to correctional mental institutions.

Activity
Carry out research and discuss if and how attitudes to the following have changed over time:

- Anorexia
- Aids
- Pre-menstrual Tension
- Post-natal Depression

- TB
- Hysteria
- Lung Cancer
- Obesity.

Health is certainly a social construction when, in accordance with the **positivist approach**, we realise that social and economic conditions, like poverty, help create illness. As **Richard Wilkinson** (1998) and **Helen Epstein** (1998) have discovered, it seems the more egalitarian a society is, the healthier it is. Those people who are in control of their lives are the ones most likely to live longest. We have heard a great deal about how stressful life is at the top, but the evidence shows that it is, in fact, more stressful to be at the bottom of the hierarchy. Both Wilkinson and Epstein point to loss of community and social cohesion, as well as deprivation and poverty, as possible causes for increasing health inequalities. Indeed, health statistics do reflect *social processes*, rather than 'real' trends of health and illness. In this way, health statistics can be compared to crime statistics.

PROBLEMS OF DEFINITION

To try to define health is to try to view health in *absolute* terms. As it is, at least partly, a social construction this may not be helpful. The World Health Organisation's definition of health is 'a state of complete physical, mental and social well-being and not merely the absence of disease and infirmity'. This would exclude most of us daily when we fall short of 'complete well-being'. Are we unwell or ill when we have a headache, feel 'a bit off colour' or 'a bit down'? It certainly makes more sociological sense to see health as a *relative* concept. This means that people understand different things by it, that it can change over time and between societies, rather like the concept of deviance. Thus, the health of an individual can be judged against their gender, age, occupation and culture. In fact, as pointed out by social scientists **Dubos** and **Pines**, health is 'the ability to function effectively within a given environment'. However, according to Illich, our well-being is dependent on accepting our frailties, depressions and pains maturely in whatever environment we find ourselves. Definitions of health therefore range from the purely biological to the social to the intensely personal.

Relativist view

To see health as a relative concept in today's multi-cultural society is to recognise that, within and between societies, individuals differ in their definition of symptoms indicative of sickness, their understanding of pain and their acceptance of appropriate remedies to particular illnesses (for example, Jehovah's Witnesses reject blood transfusions and some ethnic minorities will not receive intimate examinations from persons of the opposite sex). This is an essential concept for those working in the health and social care environment, if not for us all. The sociology of health is largely an applied science and seeks to improve medical practice to alleviate human suffering (**B S Turner**, 1992). Sociology can give insights into the causes of and cures for human ailments by acknowledging that health is a social construct and a relative concept. In this way, sociology has challenged the bio-medical model, but it does not reject the importance of biology. This, according to **W. S. Rogers** (1991), is to be **ethnocentric**. According to **A.C. Twaddle** (1973), at least some ailments must have a biological reality and cause, which places limits on interpretation. It may be an academic luxury or an indulgence to be a relativist living in the affluent West, when in Third World countries the biological reality of sickness, famine and high morality rates is ever present.

Study point

1 In what ways might it be helpful or harmful to think of health and illness as relative concepts?
2 Can health and illness be seen as purely a biological phenomenon?
3 Our ideas about health and illness have not remained static. Is a definition, therefore, possible or desirable?

THEORETICAL EXPLANATIONS OF VARIATIONS

VARIATION WITHIN AND BETWEEN SOCIETIES

Some sociologists have suggested that the biological explanations of disease should be replaced with sociological ones. However, others have been more interested in trying to explain *how* certain physical and biological states, and behaviours have come to be defined as 'healthy' or 'ill'. The distinction has been made, therefore, between disease and illness: disease is the *objective medical concept* defined by raised blood pressure, high temperature etc (with health as the absence of disease); illness is a persons' *subjective experience* of ill-health and is recognised by that person not experiencing well-being or being unable to function socially. These subjective experiences are themselves shaped by social norms and values that vary over time between and within cultures. Using the above definitions, disease and illness can occur together in a person's experience, or may not. Referring to Table 2 this becomes evident. Sometimes the status of ailments such as ME (myalgic encephalomyelitis), CJD (Creutzfeldt-Jakob Disease), PMS (pre-menstrual syndrome) falls into the 'minus illness' – 'illness' status section, but may move into the 'plus illness' status over time.

Table 2: *Illness status*		
	DISEASE +	DISEASE −
+ ILLNESS STATUS	Classic cases such as tonsillitis and measles	Women who became pregnant in the late nineteenth and early twentieth centuries Dissidents in old USSR Slaves diagnosed as having 'Drapetomentia'
− ILLNESS STATUS	CJD Gulf War Syndrome ME	The 'healthy'

In some societies there is a hierarchy of illnesses. In many Western 'science-dominated' societies of the twentieth century, some illnesses seem to be 'in the mind'. These psychological ailments are often given lower esteem than truly provable biological malfunctions or disease. It is sometimes difficult to lose the label of 'nervous breakdown sufferer', whereas such a stigma does not remain if one has suffered pneumonia. There is also a hierarchy amongst illnesses with social stigmas being attached to those seen as 'self-inflicted'. Sometimes this threatens the treatment received by the individual. Thus, people who smoke may be seen as bringing lung cancer upon themselves. Those who are homosexual, or who are heterosexual and have more than one sexual partner, are seen as bringing Aids upon themselves. Thus, medical experts have become increasingly powerful in determining how people should behave, in fact as acting as part of social control.

Study point
Using CD-Roms, the Internet, books and the media, research these questions. 1   Why has ME been so difficult to recognise as an illness? 2   How and why have the medical profession changed their minds over ME? 3   What do the answers to questions 1 and 2 tell us about how we define health and illness?

POINTS OF EVALUATION

1 Concepts of what constitutes ill health, therefore, differ between cultures depending on their environments, ideas about gender and sexuality, and what is taken for a state of 'well-being' or health.

2 In the past, people in Britain would have accepted loss of movement, hearing and eyesight as a normal part of ageing. Today we are taught that these are symptoms which can be remedied by hip replacement, hearing aids and operations for glaucoma. They have become, therefore, states of ill health. But in many Third World countries these remedies are not available and these conditions are still regarded as a normal part of ageing.

3 Studies carried out by the WHO say that more than two-thirds of people living in urban areas in Third World countries draw their water from sources which fail to meet even the most minimal health standards. 'Safe' water supplies, it has been estimated, would eradicate or cut by half 17 out of the 25 main water related diseases in Third World nations. However, these ailments are seen as part of the normal health experiences of these people.

4 Women were expected to be in almost permanent states of pregnancy or nursing in the nineteenth century (and in some countries still), but today this is seen as being deleterious to female health.

Even within industrialised societies there are major differences in the distribution of disease. About 70 per cent of deaths in Western countries are due to four major types of illness:

- cancer
- heart disease
- stroke
- lung disease.

In Chapter 4 the issues of class, gender, ethnicity and age will be examined more closely to understand these variations. Sociological research into these areas can help us to understand, not only the impact of deprivation, but also the influence of cultural norms and mores.

Activity

Find out about the norms and mores surrounding the following practices:

- circumcision (male and female)
- slimming (in West)
- bound feet (in China)
- cosmetic plastic surgery
- body piercing
- elongation of ear lobes and lip plates.

How might these practices affect health and how are they justified by the cultures in which they are found?

There are vast variations in the experience of health and ill health between and within societies. This is due, in part, to the very different ideas that exist about health and disease. These include knowledge and theories of biology, notions about the role of hygiene, the importance of pollution, the role of the 'mind' and even what is seen as moral or immoral. If there are variations in deciding what is ill health, there are certainly also variations on theories of treatments. Ideas about health and illness are being created, passed on and recreated in the light of increasing knowledge and the development of 'new' diseases, as well as the re-emergence of 'old' diseases, such as TB (tuberculosis). Health and illness are therefore, dynamic, relative concepts.

This is not to deny the reality of the biological sciences, but sociology does try to add to the whole picture of human health and, thus, contribute to answering the questions:

- Why do some people become ill?
- How will their illness affect them and their society?
- What are the treatments that will enable recovery?

Different cultures provide different answers, due to their different interpretation of health and illness. It is different ideas about how the body works that have led to alternative medicine – homeopathy and chiropractitioners for example. Chinese acupuncturists believe the body has a system of energy channels unknown in Western science. Hindu practitioners of Yoga believe the body houses a number of chakras (energy centres), also not recognised by Western science. These are considered to be successful treatments. Many millions of people have faith in them and a greater understanding of them could help to answer some of the questions.

Activity

Find out about alternative health 'cures' such as homeopathy, aromatherapy, acupuncture, osteopathy and chiropractic, and make a presentation to the rest of your class.

Study point

1 Is it possible to be ill and yet be considered by society to be healthy, or vice versa?
2 Concepts of health and illness differ between cultures. Why is this?

MEASURING HEALTH AND ILLNESS

MORBIDITY AND MORTALITY

As it is impossible to construct a universally accepted definition of health, it may seem to be equally impossible to measure health with any reliability or validity. Sociologists have similar problems when it comes to crime, suicide or, indeed, anywhere that statistics are used to define the human condition. This does not mean that we should not attempt to identify trends and the incidence of illness. To help identify levels of health and illness, we usually use two indicators: **morbidity** and **mortality**. Morbidity refers to illness and mortality refers to death.

Morbidity is potentially the most hazardous incidence to measure because it is subjective, as we have found. For example, one may have an illness – hypertension or schizophrenia – but not feel ill, or feel ill without having a specific disease. As we have already seen, 'sickness' is a social state: those who are officially sick have a social role and are an expected to seek the advice of a professional health care authority. Therefore mortality is more commonly used to study differences within and between societies.

DEPRIVATION AND HEALTH

Measurements have shown a close correlation between *economic deprivation* and *health*. The poorest countries have the highest mortality rates and, within the UK, the poorest people in the most deprived areas have higher mortality rates than their wealthier counterparts. This was shown in the BBC *Panorama* programme 'Dead Poor' televised on February 2 1995, but it is not a new idea. The Black Report 1980 (see Chapter 4) which was an inquiry into class links between health and occupation, found that men from Social Class V (unskilled manual workers) were 2.5 times more likely to die before retirement age than ones from Social Class I (professional/managerial). Table 3 shows that infant mortality is also linked to the family's social class.

Table 3: *Infant mortality*[1] *by social class*[2]			
UNITED KINGDOM	RATES PER 1000 LIVE BIRTHS [3]		
	1981	1991	1994
Professional	7.8	5.0	4.5
Managerial and technical	8.2	5.3	4.5
Skilled non-manual	9.0	6.3	5.1
Skilled manual	10.5	6.3	5.5
Semi-skilled	12.7	7.1	6.4
Unskilled	15.7	8.2	6.8
Other	15.7	12.4	8.8
All social classes	10.4	6.4	5.4

[1] Deaths within one year of birth. [2] Based on occupation of father. [3] Inside marriage.
SOURCE: SOCIAL TRENDS 27, 1997)

The Health Divide

The Health Divide (Whitehead, 1987) showed health inequality was tending to increase rather than decrease. This is discussed in more detail in Chapter 4 (see page 42–49). That we continue to attempt to measure health and illness is obviously important, as these trends need to be explained and addressed whenever possible. The sociology of health serves to focus attention on these inequalities and propose policy suggestions for the eradication of suffering (see Chapter 7).

The attempted measurement of health and illness has also illustrated the limits of medical intervention. The work of **McKeown** (1979) has shown that, despite the prestige of modern medicine, improvements in medical care account for only a relatively minor part of the decline in mortality rates before the present century. The decline was due to more effective sanitation, better nutrition, improved hygiene and the more efficient control of sewage during the late nineteenth and early twentieth centuries. This was before antibiotics, which only became available in the 1930s and 40s, were used to treat bacterial infections. Immunisations (particularly for Polio) were developed later still. Mortality rates had begun to decline long before this. Indeed, the over prescription of antibiotics is held responsible for the antibiotic resistance developed by some strains of bacteria. Illich, among others, would point out that over use and incorrect use of drugs has led to **iatrogenic** illnesses (allergies and addiction for example) so, although there is a correlation between improving health and longevity and the increase in medical knowledge, there is evidence that this is not necessarily a cause and effect relationship.

It can be seen from McKeown's work that attempts to measure health and illness may add to our understanding and dispel apparent 'common sense' views on the role of medicine in eradicating disease. Social research into health is open to the same criticisms and debates that apply in other areas of research. One of the difficulties in measuring the incidence of illness lies in what conditions are held to be illnesses and what conditions are held to be physical or mental.

Study point
1   Is it possible to measure morbidity?
2   Is it possible to obtain any objective factors concerning human health?

OBTAINING DATA TO MEASURE HEALTH

There are questions of how we obtain objective data, taking into account the different definitions of health and illness, the ethical and practical constraints and the difficulties in interpreting the data available.

In 1967 **Holmes** and **Rahe** published a table of stress factors (see Table). It attempted to quantify the amount of stress involved in a range of life events. A score of 300 points or more over a 12 month period is considered high and an indication of ill health. Most people can cope with up to 150 points over 12 months.

Table 4: *Holmes/Rahe Stress Scale*			
KEY LIFE EVENTS	POINTS	KEY LIFE EVENTS	POINTS
Death of husband or wife	100	Major change of work	39
Divorce	73	Large mortgage taken on	31
Marital separation	65	Starting a new school	26
Jail sentence	63	Leaving school	26
Illness or injury	53	Change in residence	20
Marriage	50	Change in sleeping habits	16
Loss of job	47	Major change in eating pattern	15
Retirement	45	Holiday	13
Pregnancy	40	Christmas	12
Sex problem	39	Minor violation of law	11

See how stressful your life is! Discuss the drawbacks of trying to measure stress.

Changing Illnesses

Illnesses come and go according to the occupations that people follow. Today, few people complain of Fossejaw (matchmakers complaint) and we do not have many 'Hatters' that are mad. Hat-makers, inhaling the fumes of the chemical of their trade, often in the past displayed such symptoms. Nowadays we have pollutant related illnesses (eg asthma) and have found increased ill health in people living near or working in nuclear reprocessing plants. Illness and health are demonstrably relative and changing and therefore most illusive to measurement.

SUMMARY

Defining health and illness is no simple matter. They are changing concepts which are partly socially and partly biologically constructed. They, therefore, defy absolutist attempts at measurement.

Group work

Discuss what it means for each of you to be healthy. See if you can compile a list of 12 statements concerning good health. Which of these are:

- mainly physical?
- mainly mental?
- mainly social?

Do you think your statements fit the bio-medical model?

Exam hints

Health and illness must be seen as conditions which are socially defined. Examine the evidence for this view?

This essay will require you to consider the various definitions of both health and illness. This should include a historical and cross-cultural analysis of the concepts, along with evidence which suggests a more physiological view. Your points should, as always, be backed up with relevant research examples. You could discuss Zola here (see Chapter 3) to demonstrate how negotiable illness is.

You could conclude with reference to the relative nature of health and illness and the importance of the interaction with the biological/scientific approach, which, in turn, is dependent on the state of our knowledge.

Practice questions

1 Despite many attempts it is not possible to have a definition or measurement of health or illness. Why is this?
2 Critically examine the view that improvements in the health of modern Western societies are the result of better health care.

Coursework suggestions

1 Investigate what people take to be health and illness; conduct an attitude survey on a particular illness.
2 Conduct a survey into 'who cares for the ill' in the family, with particular reference to dual-career families.
3 Conduct a victim survey of the ill on how they felt doctors, family, friends, and work place treated them. Compare a traditional illness, eg 'flu, with a socially suspect one, eg ME or backache.

3

THE SOCIOLOGICAL CONTEXT
OF HEALTH

Introduction

THIS CHAPTER WILL focus on the sociological perspectives of health and will set the scene for later chapters. It will consider the Functionalist approach; Conflict approaches (Neo-Marxist, Feminist, Radical Critique), Interactionist/Social Constructionist views, as well as post-modernism and the new realist approach. These will be considered alongside alternative and complimentary medicine. Themes throughout this chapter include the role of medicine in the decline of disease, the development of modern medicine, professionalisation of the discipline and challenges to this autonomy.

The key issue that will be explored in this chapter will focus on three themes:

- The sociological perspectives.
- Medicine as social control.
- Challenges to medical autonomy (alternative medicine).

THE SOCIOLOGICAL PERSPECTIVES

THE BIO-MEDICAL MODEL

This perspective has been touched on in Chapter 2 and is, strictly speaking, not a sociological approach. It is a model that has dominated medicine up to the present day and was developed from researchers such as **Pasteur** and **Koch** who isolated the bacillus causing TB. As a result of this there ensued a search for the

\multicolumn{4}{c}{Table 5: *Theorists, concepts and issues in this chapter*}
KEY THEORIST(S)	THEORY	KEY CONCEPTS	KEY ISSUES
Koch	Bio-medical model	The body as a machine which breaks down and needs repair – biological aspects of illness are all important	• Individuals need to be cured by medical practitioners of episodic bouts of organic disorders
Talcott Parsons	Functionalist	The 'sick role'. Illness is a form of deviance which is threatening to society. Social aspects of illness are more important than the biological.	• By adopting the sick role, individuals are allowed not to perform their normal social roles only if they agree to give themselves over to the care of a medical practitioner in order to recover
Navarro	Neo-Marxist	Definitions of health and illness are closely related to the needs of Capitalism for a healthy workforce	• State health services legitimise 'caring capitalism' and this creates a belief that medical science can provide solutions to what are really the inequalities of capitalism
Burger, Luckmann, Zola	Interactionism or Social Constructionism	Illness is socially constructed	• Ill-health is determined by an interaction of the individual's subjective experience, the cultural concept of the sick role and the medical practitioner
Doyal, Showalter Witz, Martin Oakley	Feminist	Bio-medicine legitimises female inequality	• The male domination of the bio-medical model works to women's disadvantage, medically, socially and culturally
Illich	Anti-medical model	Modern medicine creates illness	• Illness in industrial societies is iatrogenic
Sheeran	New Realism	The strengths of the bio-medical model should not be ignored for purely ideological arguments	• Socialists should utilise both subjective information (how people feel) and objective information (medical science) for overall validity
Foucault Baudrillard	Post-modernism	Bio-medicine is itself socially created knowledge	• Science is increasingly mistrusted and offers only one explanation of ill-health – people have access to a variety of models of health from which they can, and do, choose
Beck Giddens	Reflexive Modernity	Modern society is dominated by risk – especially where human diet and health are concerned	• There needs to be a coming together of science and informed reason to cope with the riskiness now inherent in every part of our global society and which has repercussions for the future

'germs' which cause illnesses and the subsequent belief that once these were isolated, then cures could be found. Thus the bio-medical model has at its core the belief that there is always a *cure*, coupled with a stress on *individuals* becoming ill. There is the idea that illness is temporary, **episodic** and **organic**, a physical condition, that cure lies solely in drugs or surgery and that this model has resulted in a decline in disease.

This view can be contrasted with the view that illness and death are integral parts of normal societies, that illness can derive from social or economic circumstances, that many illnesses are long term and/or progressive and, finally, that cures should look at the person as a whole.

POINTS OF EVALUATION

1 This model has undoubtedly led to the alleviation of much disease and, through research, is still doing so. However this model fails to consider the whole person.
2 Stress, pollution and the working environment may all affect the health of the individual.
3 It also fails to consider the day-to-day ailments that people put up with without going to a doctor.
4 It fails to explain why different societies show different patterns of health and illness.
5 Finally, evidence shown by McKeown (1979) indicates that improvement in the health of the masses was due more to improved sanitation and clear water rather than medical developments. Lower mortality and morbidity rates were in evidence before the introduction of antibiotics (by Lister) and vaccinations (by Jenner) in the nineteenth century.

Study point

Continue working on your vocabulary and find out the definitions of:

• chronic illness
• episodic disorders
• epidemic
• acute illness.

Make sure you understand the meaning of morbidity, mortality and iatrogenic, the definitions of which you will find in Chapter 2.

Changes in the Bio-medical Model

Having previously dismissed alternative medical practices as fads, in 1993 the British Medical Association or BMA responded to the changing climate of ideas and suggested that practitioners of chiropractic, herbalism, homeopathy and acupuncture should be registered. The medical profession is increasingly seeing the need to treat people holistically. The physical effects of stress are now commonly recognised and there is a less clinical approach in the treatment of terminal illness and childbirth. Over the last 20 to 30 years, hospitals have become increasingly flexible about visiting times and now allow parents to stay in hospital with their children. **Fischer** and **Warde** (1994) have pointed out the almost complete integration of osteopathy with conventional practice. In the USA and in France, 80 per cent of homeopathic medicine is supplied on prescription. Although the bio-medical model is still dominant, it may be true to say that some 'alternative' models are becoming 'complimentary'.

Activity

Try to remember the last time you visited a doctor.

1 What questions were you asked?
2 What did you think the doctor wanted you to say?
3 Were there things you didn't tell him/her but would have liked to?
4 Were you examined?
5 Was the examination general or concerned with your complaint?
6 Were you offered a prescription or choice of treatment?
7 Did you leave with a prescription?

To what extent do your experiences with doctors and other health professionals conform to me bio-medical model or reflect the changes in the bio-medical model?

THE FUNCTIONALIST PERSPECTIVE

The functionalist approach derives from **Talcott Parsons** for whom anyone who is ill is unable to perform their social roles. This has serious consequences for the functioning of society. If everyone were sick, then society would no longer function. However, Parsons suggests that illness may not be random – that there is some degree of conscious or sub-conscious desire to be sick. Thus, Parsons links the subjective experience of ill-health with the social experience to reproduce the '**sick role**'. Ill-health is, in some respects, fulfilling a defined and functional role. Parsons outlined the rights and responsibilities of the sick person. The person is, by right, exempt from nominal responsibilities such as work and can be pampered by a sympathetic carer. But this is dangerous and could lead to a subculture of 'sickness' to which people are attracted because of the release of responsibilities. Therefore, Parsons outlined the responsibilities of the 'sick role'. These are to seek professional help and to demonstrate a desire to get well. Patients who don't do this may forfeit the sympathy of others and may pass from the 'sick role' to the role of malingerer.

Parsons went on to examine other consequential characteristics of the sick role. There is the compliance and powerlessness of the patient in the patient–doctor relationship and the duty of the doctor to sort out the real cases of sickness from the work and responsibility shy. Parsons sees this as a positive, socially desirable and therefore functional role of the medical profession: doctors deal with the deviant 'sick' who are no longer satisfying their normal responsibilities.

Activity
Carry out a mini survey using questionnaires and/or interviews and observation to discover how family, friends, employers and colleagues react to people when they have had one or more of the following ailments. What were they allowed to do and what were they prevented from doing when they were ill? Did this differ from illness to illness?

- 'flu
- bad cold
- bad back or slipped disc
- tonsillitis

- broken limb
- migraine
- period pain (dysmenorrhoea)

POINTS OF EVALUATION

Parsons, through his functionalist analysis, was amongst the first to recognise the significance of the social expectations that go along with being ill. He demonstrated that a biological analysis alone is inadequate. However there are five main criticisms of this view:

1 The functionalist perspective relies too heavily on the 'over-socialised' concept of humanity (Wrong, 1969). Not everyone accepts that there is a sick role; not everyone will play by the rules and adopt the rights and responsibilities of the role. Some people will refuse to see themselves as ill and will soldier on regardless. Many disabled people do this, as do many AIDS sufferers. Some may try to hid their condition due to the stigma attached to a particular disease.

2 There has been a shift from episodic acute illness to chronic (long-term) illness during the twentieth century, so the assumption that one of the

responsibilities of the sick role is to get better, may not be realistic. The sick role is only beneficial in some cases, therefore.

3 Many ill people may not adopt the passive role. As in the case of AIDS sufferers, they may actively join together to challenge doctors and to demand their rights.

4 Parsons assumes that the sick role status is one that can be exploited by the 'ill' person. But it could also be argued that the sick are themselves exploited, not only by doctors, but by medical companies, health insurance companies and patent medicine manufacturers. **Hart** (1985) points out that the Functionalist passive view of illness ignores the 'social control' function of the medical profession. Interactionists have responded to this criticism by pointing out that the doctor–patient relationship is a *negotiated* one. There are instances where patients have refused to accept doctors' diagnoses.

5 Lastly, there are some illnesses which are seen as the fault of the individual. Smokers are considered responsible for their lung cancers or heart disease, and AIDS sufferers are often denied the rights of the 'sick role', due to their apparently socially irresponsible lifestyles. In these cases the sick role is not legitimated and rights to care may be withdrawn.

Activity

Find out the procedure in a school, college or a place of work in which they seek to legitimate illness. Does this procedure back up Parson's 'sick role'?

NEO-MARXIST PERSPECTIVE

Vincente Navarro (1978) argues that the bio-medical approach to illness undermines the freedom of the individual and serves to preserve the interests of the ruling class. In fact, neo-Marxists argue that capitalism makes people ill and, furthermore, that doctors are the gatekeepers who define who is able or unable to work. Their role is, therefore, as **agents of social control**. In a capitalist society, sickness is defined as the inability to work and those not clearly defined as ill may be seen as malingerers or deficient in their jobs, rather than unwell.

The medical profession is seen as a major consumer of the products of capitalism. The high-tech medicine we have today requires a massive industry in terms of equipment and investment into drugs research. Marxists would point out that, although many laws attempt to protect the public, non-compliance with these health, safety and equality laws can have serious effects; for example, pollution or the deaths of workers, passengers or consumers. However, 'offenders' are protected by the powerful. Each year more than 500 workers die in work-related accidents and 18,000 suffer major injuries. The Health and Safety Executive have estimated that as many as two out of three fatal accidents are attributable to violations of the Health and Safety at Work Act. Few employers are prosecuted as **Celia Wells** points out (1993). These offences may be committed by large corporations or small businesses. Danger arises out of a conflict between the need to make a profit and the requirements of safety or quality standards.

Furthermore, neo-Marxism points out that the population is duped by the bio-medical model into believing a drug or an operation can provide the answers and solutions to problems that are really produced by the inequalities of capitalism. So that medical treatment is offered, for example, to people who are depressed or stressed and to those who have emphysema, when both these conditions are related to occupation.

Although McKeown's evidence indicates that industrialisation actually improved the health of the masses, albeit due to social reformers such as **Chadwick** (whose campaigns for clear water led to the virtual elimination of typhoid and cholera), this is interpreted by neo-Marxists as legitimising '**caring capitalism**'. They also affirm that this 'care' was only sufficient to maintain the health of the working population, and so was to the benefit of the owners of the means of production. Neo-Marxists would point to the fact that, when health insurance was introduced by the Liberal government at the beginning of the twentieth century, the only people who were to receive medical treatment free of charge were the (usually male) employed head of the household, reflecting the need to keep the breadwinner working. This perspective would also point out that, despite extensive Health and Safety regulations, today firms are rarely prosecuted.

It has also been argued by neo-Marxists that capitalist production methods are unhealthy because it is too expensive to protect workers. Pollution involves incalculable costs. Illegal factory emissions and river pollution poison wildlife and affect people (Croall, 1992) but measures to prevent pollution by firms are claimed to be too expensive.

Neo-Marxists would cite examples such as these as evidence of the real, uncaring, profit conscious face of capitalism:

- In February 1999 Monsanto received a meagre £17,000 fine for leaking genetically modified pollen into the atmosphere, a potentially dangerous 'accident' for mankind.
- Corporate 'dumping' took place after the Dalkoi Shield intra-uterine device killed at least 17 women in the United States. It was withdrawn from the American market, but sold overseas for many years (Croal, 1992).
- Depo-Provera, the injectable contraceptive banned in the USA because it caused malignant tumours in beagles and monkeys, was sold by the Up John Company in 70 other countries and was widely used in US sponsored population control programmes (Simon and Eitzen, 1993).

- The drug Thalidomide, with its disastrous effects on children, continued to be sold in the Third World countries for many years after it was banned in the West.

Doyall and **Pennell** pointed out in 1979 that housework is not only unhealthy, but is also alienating. It is seen to benefit the capitalist system: housewives enable the workforce to perform their tasks by caring for them and by producing the future work force. Doyall and Pennell believe that even *not* working is a cause of illness, be it stress-related, poverty-related or leading to suicide or self-harm.

POINTS OF EVALUATION

1 Evidence *does* support the idea that greater inequality leads to poorer health in the working classes and visa versa. During the two World Wars, Britain was at it's most egalitarian and average national life expectancy increased by more than 6 years in both periods.

However:

2 The neo-Marxist perspective neglects other important variables such as gender, age and ethnicity.
3 There was disease and illness before capitalism and disease and illness existed within Marxist states.
4 Neo-Marxism neglects the fact that many illnesses are due to medical reasons.

Study point
How do you think a Functionalist would view plastic surgery? Would this differ from a Marxist's view?

FEMINISM

Feminists believe that the other perspectives fail to consider the particular experience of women within bio-medicine. Women were key to the rise of bio-medicine during the nineteenth century. However, **Doyal** (1995) has shown how the development of the medical professions has involved the wrenching of medical know how away from women by men. Women then became the 'helpers' in a male-dominated profession. This exclusion was further developed, so **Witz** (1992) points out, by men using strategies to limit women's access to medical schools. Midwives had to be supervised by doctors. Childbirth and pregnancy became defined as medical complaints. More recently, women were seen, so feminists say, as reproductive units who were made to feel guilty of risking the lives and well-being of their unborn children if they wanted to have their children at home. Even though midwifery is still mainly female, obstetricians and gynaecologists are generally male. Obstetricians tend to see pregnancy as a medical problem, whereas women see it as natural (Oakley, 1981). According to feminists, inductions of births and caesarian operations are often seen as a matter of convenience for hospitals, rather than for the good of mother and baby.

Radical feminists see bio-medicine as legitimising inequalities and controlling women. The Victorian disorder 'hysteria' was increasingly diagnosed between 1870 and 1914. This, strangely, coincided with the rise in women's movements and as **Showalter** (1991) pointed out, illustrates how a wish for privacy, independence and assertiveness amongst 'hysterics' was seen and diagnosed as abnormal by patriarchal psychologists. Modern feminists see similarities in the diagnosis of PMS and menopausal 'psychological problems'. This, they think, is another means by which men continue to demonstrate that women are controlled by their biology, whereas men are rational beings and therefore superior.

The feminist perspective points to a society that has focused women's minds on their bodies. Feminists place women's need to control their bodies so as to please men, at the centre of the reasons for the eating disorders, such as anorexia and bulimia that are most likely to affect young women. They also question why the majority of contraceptive advice is directed at women, whereas male contraceptive measures have fewer side effects and yet are not so widely used.

Study point
Discuss these questions: • Is infertility an illness? • Is the medicalisation of infertility an advantage to professional health practitioners or to 'patients'?

EVALUATION POINTS

1 Infant mortality rates and deaths of women in childbirth have reduced substantially during the late nineteenth and twentieth centuries.
2 'Prevention; of women's ailments is now accepted, whereas male killers such as prostate cancer are not publicised and do not have screening measures, such as routine cervical smears and mammograms for women.
3 There has been a rise in the number of female doctors, and midwives have become the lead professions in the management of normal deliveries.

OTHER CONFLICT APPROACHES

As mentioned in chapter 2, Ivan Illich suggests that modern medicine actually *creates* illness: he sees modern society as creating dependence of individuals on experts and technology. Illich argues that professionals are essentially self-interested groups and that technology impoverishes the individual. He proposes that iatrogenic, or treatment-caused, diseases now bring about more suffering than the combination of traffic and industrial accidents. He thinks that pain and illness have become technical problems instead of personal challenges. Illich says that he is not opposed to the use or development of new medicines, but rather he is against the domination of professionals and the mystification of their skills.

Illich identifies three kinds of iatrogenesis:

- **Clinical iatrogenesis** – resulting from harmful medical intervention such as poor surgery, addiction to drugs and the side effects of drugs (for example the 1960s Thalidomide drug which caused deformities in babies born to mothers taking it for morning sickness).
- **Social iatrogenesis** – which includes the medicalisation of natural processes such as pregnancy and childbirth. Modern social problems such as abortion and surrogacy are included here as they are dealt with by doctors rather than by society at large.
- **Cultural iatrogenesis** – which means that individuals give up their independence and allow experts to control their lives (here we allow professionals to make decisions for us).

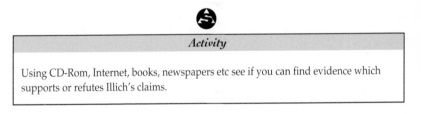

Activity

Using CD-Rom, Internet, books, newspapers etc see if you can find evidence which supports or refutes Illich's claims.

A similar approach to Illich's was taken in 1908 by **Ian Kennedy**. In that year's series of Reith Lectures, under the title of 'Unmasking Medicine', Kennedy described doctors as 'new magicians and priests wrapped in the cloak of science and reason'. Kennedy, like many others, would prefer to see medical science mainly focused on prevention, improving health education and paying more attention to the disadvantaged groups in society. It is interesting to note that, at a time when the scientific approach to sociology is out of favour and environmentalists are pointing to the pollution and devastation caused by scientific and technological changes, medical science, also, should be under attack.

INTERACTIONIST (SOCIAL CONSTRUCTIONIST) APPROACH

The concept of illness as a social creation can loosely be related to the interactionist approach. Interactionists such as **Zola** suggest that there are three stages which can be applied to health – be it bodily or mental illness. These are:

- **recognition**
- **definition**
- **action**.

Zola said that many of us *feel* ill, but that we often account for this by saying that it is due to 'growing pains', 'the damp weather', 'our age' and so on. There comes a point, however, when a person recognises that a problem exists and then defines it as an illness or complaint. This usually comes when we can no longer perform our obligations – this is the *recognition* stage. The doctor's role comes in to play at the *definition* stage. Here the doctor may well be concerned with keeping interaction with the patient as short as possible, making a diagnosis and suggesting a course of *action*.

The outcome of the doctor–patient interaction is one, therefore, of *negotiation* which, as interactionism is always keen to point out, reflects the *relative power* of the people involved. Thus it is, according to social constructionists, why middle class people and those who know how the system works, are more likely to obtain medical services than the working class (Ferrie et al, 1995).

Social constructionists, therefore, have focused their research on questioning the validity of statistics, as well as the inequalities in access to health care (Cartwright and O'Brien, 1976; Dr J Tudor-Hart). In particular, social constructionists have looked at gender and health, ethnicity and health, class and health, and age and health (see Chapter 4).

POINTS OF EVALUATION

1 Interactionists like Zola, Berger and Luckmann have looked at how mortality and illness cannot be explained in biological terms alone and have explored how social functions like class and environment affect health. In so doing they have opened up the debate within and outside sociology, which has led to many further developments in thought, such as New Realism, post-modernism etc.
2 Sheeran (1995) says that this argument has been taken to extremes. She asks, 'Is illness *only* a social construction?'

Activity
See if you can find accounts or media coverage of ill people having their right to treatment questioned or withdrawn. What reasons are given? What does this tell us about the social construction of illness?

NEW REALISM

Sheeran summarises the social construction view as follows:

1 It is based on concepts of health and illness that vary, both cross-culturally and historically.
2 The medical profession imposes its bio-medical definitions of illness on society.
3 Illness can be compared to deviance, especially where mental illness is concerned.
4 Social conditions help create illness.
5 Official statistics reflect power relations in society, rather than the real incidence of health and illness.

Sheeran goes on to criticise the relativist point of view that the bio-medical model is no more relevant or valid than other models of health. She asserts that, although we may research and focus on the social and power structures in the provision of health care, we should not ignore the great strengths of bio-medicine. The bio-medical model is based on rigorous scientific procedures. Sheeran advocates a coming together of: (1) the social constructionist view with (2) the post-modern view (which in turn places social constructionism in its socio-historical context) with (3) the recognition of the existence of objective biological conditions (diseases), in order to develop a new realist approach in sociology to health and illness. Sociology should utilise data from the medical sciences *and* information on how people feel to consider the overall validity of any data.

POST-MODERNISM

The post-modernism view is that we are now living through a revolution from which post-modernism itself has sprung, fuelled by advances in technology and in global news media. The post-modernist view is that contemporary society is intrinsically fragmented and dynamic. **Baudrillard** (1988) argues that, in this fluid situation, science is increasingly mistrusted in its ability to solve problems. The Industrial Revolution led to a rise in science and a belief in the bio-medical model of health. This second revolution is characterised by a denial of science as 'truth'. People now have access in the world of news communications to a huge variety of models of health from which they can choose. Consumers now buy into or out of private health care, state health care, alternative medicine, whatever. Post-modernists argue that no single theory or meta-theory can reduce all experiences to the biomedical view of illness. They see bio-medicine as socially created knowledge and of no more worth than any other theory. Post-modernists do not try to decide which approach is best – they are more interested in the way in which dominant bio-medical explanations and complementary medicines attempt to gain status and power over others. In other words, all theories are just ideas which compete to become recognised in the (illusory) truth.

The influence the biomedical model has had, according to post-modernists, is due to dominant discourses which reflect power structures within society. In this case the power structures see one type of knowledge (medical) as superior to another (say–magic). As **Michael Senior** (1996) says, possessors of this (powerful) knowledge can then exercise control over others; doctors claim that their knowledge of the body is superior to their patients. In this way language affects thinking. This is known as **discourse**.

Dominant medical discourse has medicalised human conditions such as being overweight (obesity), being sad (depression) or being worried (anxiety). This medical scientific discourse shapes the way people view society.

According to Foucault, knowledge cannot be separated from power, so definitions of health and illness depend on who has the power to define the state our body is in. In Medieval times this might have been the priest, nowadays it is the doctor.

Post-modernists like **Fox** (1993) treat all sociological theories as problematic and in need of 'deconstruction'. Fox has suggested that a sceptical stance is a possible way forward for the sociology of health: we should not involve ourselves with seeking the 'truth' in relation to medical knowledge as it is not possible to isolate one truth.

Study point

TB and AIDS are not just viewed as illnesses according to **Susan Sontag** (1991). People attach *meaning* to illness so that they become stigmatised by it. This may change people's self-identity – how they feel about themselves. Does the body exist in abstract? How does this fit in with post-modernist ideas?

RISK SOCIETY

Whereas a post-modern view would point to a 'pick and mix' approach to medicine, with people choosing orthodox medicine and supplementing it with alternative medicines, **Ulrich Beck's** 'Risk society' analysis has more in common with Illich and Kennedy. Beck sees 'Risk Society beginning where nature ends' (Beck, 1992).

Giddens has also talked about the riskiness involved in modern societies. One of the particularly difficult dimensions to this new riskiness, according to both Beck and Giddens, is the incalculability and unpredictability of the effects of so much modern technology. In risk society, consequently, the former 'welfare state' modes of attributing causality and allocating compension have irreversibly broken down (Beck, 1998). Furthermore, these new risks also have a way of 'colonising the future' so that 'Events that do not exist (yet) strongly influence our present affairs and actions', so much so that, 'risks are a kind of virtual, yet real, reality' (Beck, 1998). Several times Beck makes the stark observation that the injured and dying of Chernobyl are today, years after the catastrophe, still waiting to be born. This situation, however, has not come about by choice – rather it has arisen through the automatic and autonomous operations of the modernisation processes and by the science that drives it. Whereas science was once regarded as the major source of *solutions* for the problems besetting mankind, it is increasingly seen in risk society, and in risk theory, as part of the *problem* (Durant, 1998). This is not to say, however, that Beck or Giddens are merely propounding a more sophisticated version of a doom laden and fairly widespread anti-science rhetoric. For them, a critical engagement with science – especially and necessarily by it's practitioners – rather than a rejection of science, is the only constructive way forward for humankind (Beck, 1995). In this way, risk society theorists have taken Illich's critique one step further. Beck sees the answer as lying in what he terms 'radicalised' or 'reflexive modernity'. Risk society is a society of greater choices and more opportunities, more uncertainty and potentially greater dangers of making the wrong choices. It is a society without the comfort and support of the traditional family and community structures of the past.

According to much research, Britain was at its most healthy and egalitarian during the two World Wars. Life expectancy increased by more than 6 years in both periods. Government policies to improve the nation's health and the increased use of antibiotics certainly played a part, but a more egalitarian society equals a healthier society (Wilkinson, 1998). Global risk society, however, is dominated by extremes of poverty and wealth, deprivation and plenty. Helen Epstein points out (1998) that rising increases in inequalities and the collapse of trade unions which created a sense of solidarity, coupled with unemployment and rising divorce, has meant our society lacks *cohesion* – the social solidarity that Durkheim saw as so important. There is no proof as to whether any of these things are the cause of the other, but risk society may mean a potentially less healthy, less cohesive society.

This is a world where even eating becomes problematical. Technological 'advances' have thrown up problems such as the BSE (bovine spongiform encephalopathy) crisis and concern now with GE (genetically engineered) and GM (genetically modified) food products. Whereas post-modernism sees politics as at an end, 'risk society' theory sees reflexive modernisation as capable of generating a new politics of 'dialogic democracy' – or sceptical engagement with science and technology (Giddens, 1998).

Activity
In groups, see if you can agree that we live in a global risk society where health is concerned. Consider BSE, GE foods, Ebola and AIDS in the light of Risk Society theory.

MEDICINE AS SOCIAL CONTROL

Two themes running through the sociological perspectives have been the *concept of power* and the *medical profession as an agency of social control*.

- From the functionalist approach this is a positive relationship. Medicine is a dedicated profession with a body of knowledge, professional authority and the right to discipline its own members. This involves the monopoly of the provision of health care for the good of the community, a strict code of ethics and a professional culture (involving a common sense of identity and purpose).
- The Marxist approach explained by Navarro sees the doctor as an agent of social control for the benefit of the bourgeoisie. It is the doctor's job to keep the workforce healthy and to mystify people as to the real causes of illness in the world.
- The radical approach voiced by **Friedson** (1992) argues the profession exists to benefit the professionals rather than the community, by, as **Parry** and **Parry** point out, restricting entry, controlling the public image of doctors and claiming that only professional members are qualified to perform the service (thereby excluding homeopathy and alternative medicine). Illich takes this further by saying that doctors are actually responsible for a huge amount of ill-health.
- Feminists see the health profession as controlling women, both as patients and as health practitioners.
- Post-modernists see medicine as just one form of control which has gained power alongside the general rise in the power of science during the nineteenth and twentieth centuries.
- Risk theorists see scientific knowledge in the hands of policy-makers who manage risk society for the benefit of all. Up until now, science has been allowed, during modernity, to go ahead unchallenged by ethical or moral considerations.

Medical decisions have been used as 'social control', especially where mental health is concerned. Those whose behaviour the powerful do not like have, in many parts of the world, been diagnosed as unwell – be it the woman hysteric in Victorian England, the slave with drapetomania in the Southern USA, or the political dissident in the former USSR.

The medical profession, despite a growing distrust of science, still maintains a power base and therefore continues to act as a very influential agent of social control. Members of the BMA and The Royal College of Medicine have privileges envied by many other occupations: doctors have high salaries and prestige.

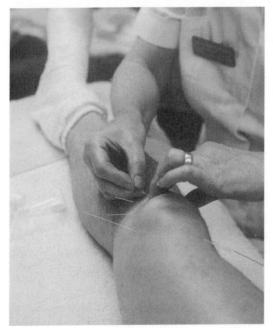

Activity
How do ideas about AIDS, stress, diet and smoking control our behaviour?

CHALLENGES TO MEDICAL AUTONOMY

Interest in traditional and alternative approaches to health have grown rapidly, with sales of alternative medicines in the UK increasing from £20.7 million in 1988 to £32.5 million in 1992. Mainstream stores such as Boots the chemist now stock alternative therapies. In Britain, there are over 100 alternative medical treatments available with over 90,000 practitioners. These treatments, especially those of Eastern origin, tend to focus on the patient as a whole person. Many claim to work by using the body's own healing powers. Others stress the use of

ALTERNATIVE THERAPIES, SUCH AS ACUPUNCTURE WHICH AIMS TO TREAT THE WHOLE PERSON, ARE BECOMING INCREASINGLY POPULAR.

natural herbal remedies. The most popular are acupuncture, homeopathy, osteopathy and herbalism. Others attracting followers are aromatherapy, reflexology, shiatsu, crystal healing and colour therapy. **Ursula Sharma** (1992), has described the ten most popular practices in descending order. These are:

1	Herbalism	6	Spiritual Healing
2	Osteopathy	7	Hypnotherapy
3	Homeopathy	8	Reflexology
4	Acupuncture	9	Naturopathy
5	Chiropractic	10	Aromatherapy.

Activity

Try to find out something about each of the alternative medicines in Sharma's list. How does this plurality of perspectives add to the argument that health is as much a social construction as a biological fact?

The populations of industrial societies seem to be becoming health 'consumers' who want, not only more information, but also more choice in health care. More people are now open to the idea of balancing the use of orthodox medicine with types of complimentary medicine.

Stephen Hunt and **Nikki Lightly** (1999) have attempted to categorise the alternative therapies into:

1 those concerned with touch and relaxation, eg reflexology
2 manipulation techniques, eg chiropractic, osteopathy
3 those concerned with energetic balances in the body, eg acupuncture
4 those based on biochemistry, eg herbal medicine
5 therapies concerned with integrating various aspects of the mind and body, eg yoga.

However, they admit that although these classifications are useful, they fail to do justice to the variety and scope of the vast range of medicines and therapies on offer.

Hunt and Lightly go on to point out that it is only the power and dominance of the medical model that gives it the authority to label these practices as 'alternatives'. It seems that people are so socialised to have faith in the dominance of bio-medicine that alternative treatments are considered to be on the fringe of respected medical practice.

Sharma investigated the issue of whether alternative medicine was just marginal, or a serious challenge to bio-medicine. She interviewed 30 people from the Stoke-on-Trent area who had used one form of alternative medicine in the past 12 months. Her sample was obtained by inviting readers of a local newspaper to volunteer their experiences. She found five main reasons why people turned to alternative medicine. They are:

1 Some people thought bio-medicine emphasised the treatment of symptoms and failed to get at the route cause of the illness.
2 Some were afraid of the addictive prospect of some drugs, the side effects and the strength of drugs that they saw as too powerful for their ailments.
3 Some felt that the treatment offered them was too radical or intensive.
4 Some thought that conventional medicine had failed to fully respect their experience of illness and its social effects.
5 Many were unhappy with the doctor–patient relationship and felt that alternative therapies gave them a more active role.

Hunt and Lightly also outline five broad interrelated reasons to explain the growth of alternatives. These are that:

1 People find it hard to accept that orthodox medicine sometimes fails and so resort to an alternative.
2 People are increasingly critical of the harmful effects of the orthodox services.
3 There is a growing dissatisfaction in people of all ages with what is available in the orthodox medical sphere (eg the long waiting lists for treatment and above all its failure to cure chronic disease).
4 Some people have religious or philosophical arguments against certain Western medical practices.
5 There is a growing proportion of the population which simply needs to be different and experiment (eg alternative medicine is part of a cultural current which embraces New Age therapies, the holistic health and wholefood movement, the quest for the 'natural' in therapy, childbirth, food and so on).

ALTERNATIVE HEALTH, CLASS, AGE, SEX AND ETHNICITY

Another way of finding out why alternatives are on the increase is to find out about the social groups and individuals who use these approaches. It was thought at one time that 'non-scientific' forms of medicine and healing were the preserve of the uneducated lower classes. However, in Britain there are more alternative patients from socio-economic grades A and B (professional, managerial, technical, business, academic etc) than from other social groups (Hunt and Lightly, 1999). It seems to be the middle classes who are more educated about what is available and who can afford to buy such alternatives.

As far as age is concerned, **Fielder** and **Monro's** (1985) survey indicates that patients of alternative practitioners tend to be predominantly young to middle aged. Most surveys in Britain, as in other countries, show that a slightly larger number of females than males use non-orthodox medicine. This may simply reflect the fact that women use orthodox practices more than men, but it may also reflect female impatience and dissatisfaction with male-dominated mainstream medicine.

The Mori Poll of 1988 showed that black people (29 per cent) in Britain were slightly less likely than white people (31 per cent) to use the most popular forms of alternative practices. Non-white people were also shown to be more likely to use homeopathy and spiritual healing methods. It would seem that ethnic groups vary considerably in the emphasis they put on orthodox or alternative forms of healing.

But are alternative medicines really alternatives? **Crawford** (1977) argues that they are not, in that they still put the emphasis in health care upon the *individual*. This ignores vital social constraints such as poor environment, occupation, social class, background and ethnic factors. Fielder (1992) does argue that alternative medicine has the advantage of being **holistic**. This means it puts an emphasis upon self-healing through dealing with the mind, body and spirit. In these ways alternative medicine could well offer a sound underpinning for improving health in society.

Sharma says that alternative medicine is not a minor issue, '... that it may well be the start of a growing antagonism to the bio-medical model'. This, in turn, may be part of the growing scepticism that science has the answer to all our problems and a burgeoning awareness that science has actually caused some of our present problems. As Fielder (1992) argues, practitioners of these alternative approaches may well be unprepared to take sole responsibility for their patients' well-being, but a future where alternatives can work with and also compliment the bio-medical model on an equal level may well be possible. The bio-medical model, in this case, may well be losing its powerful monopoly position.

SUMMARY

Despite the many different perspectives to the sociology of health and reflecting as they do different eras and different states of knowledge, there is growing agreement that each perspective adds something to our overall understanding. The way forward for sociology will be in reaffirming a commitment to improving the human lot coupled with the adaptability to take on board new ideas.

Coursework

Before you start any coursework you must be aware of the ethical issues involved in asking people about their health, especially when illnesses are concerned – these are private matters and may not be deemed to be within the bounds of sociology students' enquiries.

1 Make a survey of the extent to which people have used alternative health care. Do people pick and mix their health care? If so when, and under what conditions?
2 Look back at some attitude surveys into what people consider as health and illness in themselves and in other people. See if this has changed over time, according to gender, age, class or ethnic group.

Practice questions

1 Compare and contrast two sociological perspectives of health.
2 'Doctors have the power to label a person "ill" or "healthy".' What are the implications of this statement for an understanding of health and illness in today's society?
3 Critically assess the contributions of sociologists to an understanding of medicine as social control.
4 'Alternative health care is not really an alternative at all'. Discuss.

Group work

Your class has been asked to make a presentation to another A Level sociology group outlining the historical and theoretical development of Western ideas about health. Use OHTs and handouts where appropriate.

Exam hints

'Assess the contribution of social constructionism to the sociological understanding of health.'

In this essay the contribution of social constructionism should be firmly put into context, both historically and by considering the understanding of health before this approach was conceived. The essay could go on to point out that social constructionism took the study of health beyond the physiological, by mentioning research and authors to back this up. You could question whether this approach has been taken too far, as Sheeran suggests.

You could conclude by returning directly to the wording of the question to point out that social constructionism not only took our understanding forward, but has also led to more research, more questioning (such as Risk Society theorising) and, as such, has greatly contributed to our knowledge and hence our ability to offer constructive advice to health professionals, non-professional carers, interpreters, researchers and policy-makers.

4

HEALTH INEQUALITIES

Introduction

THIS CHAPTER EXPLORES the recent developments in ideas about health care and illness. These have increasingly acknowledged that social and environmental conditions have a profound impact upon the incidence of disease and death rates. It is, therefore, crucial to recognise how social – and other – identities, such as class, religion, gender and age play an instrumental role in influencing the risks of illness and mortality.

The key issues that will be explored in this chapter will focus on two important themes:

- The experience of different social classes, gender, ethnic and age groups with regard to mortality and morbidity rates.
- The sociological explanations that attempt to account for these differences.

HEALTH AND SOCIAL STATUS

Mortality and morbidity rates show considerable variations both between and within societies. Whilst the focus of this chapter will be on health differences that relate to the different social characteristics of groups in Britain it should not be forgotten that the mortality and morbidity rates in parts of the developing world will be very different.

Sociologists and other social investigators have demonstrated that health and ill health are connected to the social status of an individual, and that the social characteristics that a person possesses will have a demonstrable impact on the

Table 6: *Theorists, concepts and issues in this chapter*		
KEY THEORIST	KEY CONCEPTS	KEY ISSUES
The Black Report Townshend and Davidson (ed)	Marked class gradient in health	Social class inversely related to mortality and morbidity rates
The Health Divide Whitehead	Differential health experiences cannot be explained away as artefact	Widening of health inequalities between social groups
Doyal	Medicalisation of the female body	Gendered health patterns explained by social rather than biomedical causes
McNaught	Racism exists at both the personal and institutional level in the NHS	Ethnic minorities receive a poorer level of care from the NHS
Medical Research Council	Ageist practices exist within the NHS	Age is being used as the main criteria to determine whether elderly people receive medical treatment

chances of that person experiencing illness. It is clear that environmental factors, whether at work or in the home, remain crucial indices that contribute to the risks of illness and mortality. However, it must be remembered than an individual does not experience one social characteristic to the exclusion of all others and that **class**, **gender**, **ethnicity** and **age** will all combine to produce a different health experience for, say, a white, middle-class, middle-aged man and a black, working-class, young, adult woman.

Therefore, this chapter will examine the extent to which social characteristics impact upon health and illness patterns in Britain and offer a critical assessment of the contributions that sociologists have made to an understanding of the relationship that exists between social inequalities and health.

HEALTH AND SOCIAL CLASS

Of all the sites of inequality that exist between different social groups, class remains one of the most potent and the gap that exists between the rich and the poor is often seen as having a major influence upon the health of an individual.

'Class', however, is a problematic concept. Prime Ministers Margaret Thatcher, John Major and Tony Blair all signalled their intention to create a classless society in Britain. This seems to run counter to sociological evidence which suggests that class remains a crucial source of social identity in Britain, affecting the health of an individual from the cradle to the grave.

We have already discussed the problems associated with measuring health (see Chapter 2). The problem of analysing class stems from both the subjective interpretations that individuals place upon their own class and the objective attempts that have been made by sociologists and other social observers to measure it as a phenomenon. The increasingly fragmented nature of the class structure and the variety of class schema that have been developed as analytical tools raise the possibility that sociologists may discover different patterns of health inequality depending on the classification scheme that they employ.

Study point

Carry out research into the following class classification schemes:

1   The Registrar General's Scheme
2   The Erikson-Goldthorpe Scheme
3   The Surrey Occupational Class Scheme.

Many sociologists are highly critical of the Registrar General's (RG) classification scheme as it focuses largely on status which, as a very subjective concept, raises doubts about the objectivity of the entire scheme. The impreciseness of what this scale measures and how well it measures it raises serious doubts about explanations of the size and trends of social variations in health made by observers who have employed this scheme.

Consequently sociologists such as **Bartley**, **Carpenter**, **Dunnell** and **Fitzpatrick** (1996) at Nuffield College, Oxford University, advocate the use of the Erikson-Goldthorpe (EG) scheme because it offers more accurate definitions of status, skill level, income and occupational autonomy.

POINTS OF EVALUATION

1   Comparing investigations into class and health that have employed different occupational schema is difficult.
2   Most schema find it difficult to classify the unemployed, and health and unemployment is a crucial issue.
3   Most schema, apart from the Surrey Occupational Class Scale, exclude women, and gender and health is a crucial concern.

The most detailed and exhaustive information on class-related health care has been derived from two important sources:

• The Report on the Working Party on Inequalities in Health (known as the *Black Report*)
• *The Health Divide*.

The Black Report

In 1977 the Labour Government set up a Royal Commission chaired by Sir Douglas Black. It was to investigate how successful the National Health Service (NHS) had been in meeting its aims in the postwar period. Implicit in the mission of the NHS was to meet the population's health care needs, irrespective of class, age, gender and ethnicity.

The report was bleak in its findings. Using mortality rates and the RG classification scheme, it found that people in Social Class I were less likely to die than those in Social Class V, and that the rates of death in Social Classes II to IV were exponentially linked to their relative class positions. At every life stage, from infancy to old age, the occupational mortality statistics showed that a person's chance of living longer, or living at all, were directly related to their social class. This was especially pronounced when it came to the 'major' diseases – coronary heart disease, diseases of the respiratory system and strokes.

The report went on to examine the four main theoretical approaches that could explain the relationship between health and class inequality:

1 *Artefact explanations* – an artefact is something that is made by people; it is artificial, not natural. This explanation says that the gloomy connection between class and health is inaccurate. It only appears to be the case because of artificial and inaccurate statistics.
2 *Theories of natural and social selection* – people are in a lower class because of their poor health, rather than having poor health because of their class.
3 *Cultural or behavioural explanations* – these blame those with ill health for not looking after themselves properly. The causes lie in unhealthy behaviour such as excessive smoking and drinking, sedentary lifestyles and eating the wrong foods.
4 *Materialist or structural explanations* – this approach points to material factors such as low income, poor housing, smoking and drinking to relieve stress, and poor contact with help agencies as important factors in determining the poor health of the lower classes.

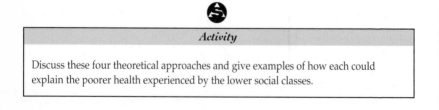

Activity

Discuss these four theoretical approaches and give examples of how each could explain the poorer health experienced by the lower social classes.

The relationship between class and ill health was clearly seen as a problematic issue. The authors of the report commented:

Choosing between such complex and sometimes competing approaches, when applied to evidence as complex as that which we have assembled, is a daunting task. We must make clear our belief that it is in some form or forms of 'materialist' approach that the best answer lies. But there can be little doubt that amongst all the evidence there is much that is convincingly explained in alternative terms: cultural, social selection and so on. Moreover it may well be that different kinds of factors, or forms of explanation, apply more strongly, or more appropriately, to different stages of the life cycle.

P. Townsend and N. Davidson, *Inequalities in Health – The Black Report* (1982)

The report concluded that there was a marked **class gradient** in health and that this appeared to be uniquely so in Britain. One of the key findings was that social class was inversely related to mortality and morbidity rates. The lower the class, the higher the rates and vice versa. Alarmingly, it was noted that people in the lower social classes were often experiencing comparatively worse health than they had 30 years before.

The report was eventually published in 1982 as *Inequalities in Health – The Black Report*, edited by **Townsend** and **Davidson**. The damning indictment it made of social inequality in Britain was rejected by the first Thatcher Government, which inherited its findings. Attempts were made to suppress and limit its publication and to play up the cultural and behavioural explanations which struck a chord with New Right notions of personal culpability when it came to social circumstances. As a result the government distanced itself from the report and refused to commit itself to any of the findings it contained.

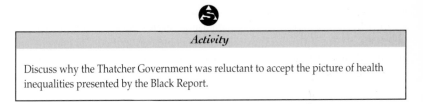

Activity

Discuss why the Thatcher Government was reluctant to accept the picture of health inequalities presented by the Black Report.

Despite determined efforts by the Government to quash the report it acted as a prompt for other sociologists to investigate the correlation between class differences and health patterns. This was a feature of key research carried out throughout the 1980s, which was collated in The Health Divide.

The Health Divide

In 1987 the Health Education Council (later renamed the Health Education Authority) published *The Health Divide – Inequalities in Health in the 1980s*. The review carried out by **Whitehead** used data collected up until 1985, thereby updating the data used as the basis for *The Black Report*. The investigation concluded that, whilst the general trend showed an improvement in the Nation's health, the gap between the classes had actually widened throughout the 1980s. Far from contradicting the original report, Whitehead discovered that the health of the lower classes had actually fallen when placed in the context of the general improvement in the health of the population. The gap between manual and non-manual workers' rates of chronic sickness rose between 1974–84, and from 1979–84 the gap also widened for acute sickness.

However, Whitehead was criticised for continuing to use the RG classification scheme. **Illsley** (1986), and **Jones** and **Cameron** (1984) criticise the RG classification system for inflating the size of the mortality and morbidity differential to the point of making comparisons meaningless. Essentially this renewed artefact theory is rejected by Whitehead who acknowledges the flaws in the RG classification system but counters by saying:

The recent evidence continues to point to the very real differences in health between social groups which cannot be explained away as artefact. On the contrary [new evidence suggests] the Registrar-General's classification may under-estimate the size of the social class gradient in health.

M. Whitehead, *The Health Divide – Inequalities in Health in the 1980s* (1987)

Whitehead's contention has been supported by **Bartley** et al (1996). Both the RG classification system and the EG scheme were used to investigate the health experiences of men employed over the period 1976–86. Whilst both schemes of classification indicated that men in unskilled and semi-skilled manual work suffered considerable health disadvantages, the EG classification indicated a *higher* risk of death for routine non-manual and service workers and a much *lower* mortality risk for agricultural workers when compared to the RG scheme. They concluded that the use of the RG scheme might actually result in an under-estimation of mortality and morbidity rates. Nevertheless, both systems still pointed to a similar conclusion – class differences underpinned health differences and any discussion on the accuracy of a given classification system does not deflect from the argument that health is based on real inequalities.

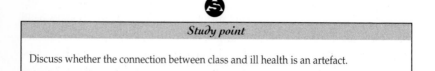

Study point
Discuss whether the connection between class and ill health is an artefact.

The fundamentalist question as to which of the models discussed in *The Black Report* best explains the connection between class and ill health remains unanswered. Sociologists have produced findings that echo many of the theoretical positions discussed in the report. Taking height as an indicator of health, Illsley's study of women in Aberdeen observed that taller women moved up a class upon marriage and shorter women moved down. Similarly Wadsworth (1986) suggested that seriously ill boys tended to suffer a fall in class. Both imply a tacit support for the social selection model. Whitehead herself noted that the strong interrelationship between the materialist explanations and the culturalist explanations had become so blurred as to make distinctions between the two approaches no longer appropriate.

However, even if explanations are elusive, the evidence still suggests that the higher social classes continue to enjoy longer life and that class differences have not diminished. Research published in the British Medical Journal (BMJ) argued that the decade of the 1980s had not witnessed any real change in this respect. **Smith**, **Bartley** and **Blane** (1990) found that, if anything, social class differences in mortality have widened and that there are clear social class differences in the quality of health enjoyed during life, as well as the length of life. Importantly, this investigation argues that the differences are apparent no matter which measure of social class is used.

Activity
Draw up a table detailing the major investigations into social class and ill health since the 1970s. List the key findings of each report.

The evidence seems compelling, indicating that the lower classes suffer more in the way of debilitating illnesses. This disadvantage seems to begin at birth, with lower-class children starting life with a lower birth rate and experiencing a greater likelihood of contracting cerebral palsy, asthma, hearing the visual impairments, as well as experiencing diet-related problems such as obesity and tooth decay.

Whilst significant, these problems seem to multiply enormously in adulthood with the working class suffering much more in the way of acute (short-term) illnesses and even more when it comes to chronic (long-term) illnesses. Once again, class cultural factors appear to play a part with the working classes under-utilising the NHS and the care agencies that could offer help. Writing in the *Lancet* in 1971, Dr Tudor-Hart identified the **'inverse care law'** in which doctors are less likely to set up a practice in a working-class area and more likely to spend extra time with middle-class patients. The working classes are less likely to ask questions of doctors and are unlikely to be able to afford private health care, where the advantages that the wealthier classes enjoy become more apparent. Private patients enjoy longer consultation periods at times more convenient to them and feel that they are being treated as a person, not as a case.

| *Study point* |

Investigate the main features of the 'inverse care law'. Discuss how far it contributes towards an understanding of the health experiences of the working classes.

Cartwright and **O'Brien** (1976) found that when it came to length of consultation, the number of questions asked and the number of problems discussed, middle-class patients on average scored more highly in each category. Later research by **Wiles** and **Higgins** (1996) found that most private patients were middle class and that they felt that paying for a consultation resulted in their being given more time and respect from the doctor.

Nettleton (1995) describes the more stressful and traumatic life events experienced by the working class and how these contribute to the greater incidence of acute and chronic illness patterns. Working-class jobs carry with them conditions in which accidents are likely, or involve a greater chance of exposure to hazardous materials. This is compounded by the greater likelihood of experiencing severe life events such as deaths, poor relationships, unemployment, loss of status, all of which can affect health. In addition, the working classes have fewer resources to draw on for help.

More recently, figures published by the Office for National Statistics have revealed that life expectancy has now stopped rising for the lower social classes. It is argued that, for the first time this century outside of war, life expectancy of women in Social Classes IV and V has remained constant and that for men in these social classes there has actually been a small decline. Whilst life expectancy amongst the other classes continued to increase, thus accounting for the *overall trend* to a greater life expectancy, for the lower classes a period of stasis or even decline has now begun.

In Liverpool in 1840, the average age of death was 35 for the gentry and professional persons, 22 for tradesmen and their families, and 15 for labourers. At that time infectious diseases were the major causes of early death. Today, male life expectancy is 74 years and it is degenerative diseases like coronary heart disease, stroke and cancer, which dominate the mortality statistics. Yet social class differences in health remain. In 1991, the male mortality rate was three times higher in Social Class V than in Social Class I. Moreover, social class differences are not diminishing: in fact, they have increased across the last two decades.

Graham (1997)

However, the class structure in Britain is far from static. Social mobility has resulted in a much more fragmented class structure in the postwar period. The percentage of people in the lower social groups is declining all the time. As the working class constricts and the middle class expands, it may eventually lead to a situation in which only a few people remain in Social Class V, yet in terms of an artefact explanation it would still be possible to discuss 'the health divide'. However, it may be the case that, as this class disappears, so does the notion of the health divide. It is arguable that health problems are beginning to traverse up the social scale. Middle-class employment no longer carries automatic job security. Short term contracts and redundancy are now of feature of the general employment landscape. The middle classes now face an uncertain future in a way once typical of the working-class experience. Unemployment or the threat of unemployment is stressful and has a knock-on effect on the health of an individual and this may witness a change in the health patterns of the middle classes.

Activity

1   Is there a health divide or is this an artefact?
2   The class structure has not remained static – have explanations of class and health?

HEALTH AND GENDER

The study of women's health offers an intriguing insight on the whole question of inequality and health. Whilst evidence suggests a marked difference in the mortality and morbidity rates of women compared to men, female symptomatology also indicates that diagnosis and treatment are often based on social criteria. Moreover, by looking at women as both patients and as workers in the health care labour force the stereotypes of sex and gender that underpin medical knowledge can be identified.

Female Mortality

In terms of mortality, women live longer than men. *The Black Report* broke down death rates by sex and by social class and in every class from I to V the death rate for women compared to men was significantly lower. Boys have a much higher mortality rate in their first year of life and records going as far back as 1838 indicate that women have always lived longer than men. Indeed, whilst life expectancy has increased for both sexes since 1900, the average life span for men is 72 years whereas the average for women is 78 years.

For women, the key factor in their longevity this century has been the reduction of deaths as a result of childbirth. Not only are women having many fewer children than at the beginning of the century, developments in medical techniques and improvements in post-natal care have resulted in a much lower mortality rate for women. Conversely, male mortality rates seem to be connected with the different lifestyle patterns than men enjoy compared to women.

WHILST LIFE EXPECTANCY HAS INCREASED FOR BOTH SEXES SINCE THE BEGINNING OF THE TWENTIETH CENTURY, THE AVERAGE LIFE SPAN FOR WOMEN IS SIX YEARS LONGER THAN FOR MEN.

Male Mortality

It is impossible to ignore the gender argument in the context of health. The prevalence of high infant mortality for boys is compounded by their experience of socialisation with its emphasis on masculine traits. In later life this makes men less likely to admit illness or to see the need to take health care precautions. Mend tend to lead more hazardous lives, take greater risks and undertake activities both at home and at work that are damaging to their health. Males have a higher propensity to parasuicidal behaviour – they drink and smoke more, drive faster and gravitate to more dangerous hobbies and social pursuits. This deliberate risk-taking that could end in death is also compounded by a much higher male suicide rate. In addition, males are more likely to be murderers and to be murdered. Indeed, the attempts by many men to live up to their gender stereotype has made their mortality rate worse as a consequence.

The Cultural Difference Between men and Women

Part of socialisation for women has involved the duty of care for others. Females tend to shoulder the burden of domestic duties and childcare as well as accepting the emotional burdens of most relationships. Female socialisation has impressed upon most women the need to take on the responsibility for others and this has been seen as a primary cause of increased stress and stress-related problems for women.

This cultural difference between men and women goes to the very nub of the nature versus nurture argument as it involves a consideration of whether women are *biologically* predisposed towards greater longevity than men, or whether these differences result from sexual stereotypes and the social construction of identity. Most sociologists would acknowledge that there may be a biological basis for the behaviour of males and females, but that this has served to underpin social stereotypes which have traditionally stressed the importance of male attributes and behaviour.

Study point
Discuss the reasons why women are more likely to visit a doctor than men.

One of the most prevalent stereotypes of femininity is the notion that women are naturally more delicate and prone to illness. This has been partly attributed to female oversensitivity about health issues, but mainly to the health problems that arise from the female reproductive system: menstruation, contraception, pregnancy and menopause.

Female morbidity

A great deal of illness and suffering is caused by diseases which are not fatal, but that are acute or chronic, and debilitating for the sufferer. At almost every life stage women, more than men, report with short and long term conditions and are more susceptible to suffer disability and strokes, rheumatoid arthritis, diabetes and varicose veins.

Trowler (1996) considers the models put forward by the authors of *The Black Report* to explain ill health (see page 44) and adds a few extra to account for female health patterns:

- *Genetic explanations* – women suffer greater morbidity owing to biological reasons. Cervical cancer is gender-specific and the stronger female immune response increases the risk of arthritis in later life. In addition, the lower mortality rate for women means that, by definition, more women than men will seek medical intervention for the diseases associated with old age.
- *Artefact explanations* – statistics are misleading. Women may seek more medical help than men, but this is often on the behalf of others, such as children and relatives. Men are not necessarily healthier than women, rather they consult doctors less than women. It may be culturally more acceptable for women to seek help, which implies an under-reporting of male morbidity.
- Stress – medical practitioners are increasingly concerned with stress and its effects on health. It triggers physiological changes once necessary for the

human 'flight or fight' response to danger. However, modern stress is not episodic like the threats that our ancestors faced. As a result stress is a long term debilitater. At work men tend to work longer, unsociable hours in areas of greater risk. Women now make up over half of the full-time workforce, but still stake primary responsibility for domestic duties and feel consequently stressed.

- *Cultural/behavioural explanations* – men have a propensity for taking risks. However, this is where class and gender collide, with more and more women beginning to smoke and drink excessively. **The Office for Population Censuses Studies** (OPCS) (1990) found that the death rate for lung-cancer deaths amongst women was 50 per cent higher in 1988 compared to 1974. The same study found that the weekly average consumption of alcohol for women rose by 14 per cent between 1978 and 1987, but fell by 4 per cent for men in the same period. Men still smoke and drink more than women, but for women the health risks associated with such activities are higher.

- *Structural/material explanations* – gender differentials in mortality and morbidity rates are derived from occupation. Work causes illness and premature death and the exclusion of women from the labour market until comparatively recently explains why the relative rates for men and women are different. Women's illness rates are linked to stress-related problems that are caused by conflicts arising from matching their perceived role to care for others to other notions concerning self-fulfilment.

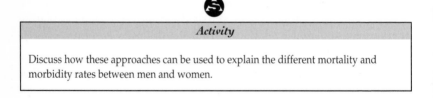

Activity

Discuss how these approaches can be used to explain the different mortality and morbidity rates between men and women.

Feminist Contributions

Feminists have been highly critical of the exclusionist tactics of the male-dominated medical profession. Doctors have alienated women from knowledge about their own bodies and have medicalised their bodies in the process. Doyal (1995) examines how men seized control of the medical profession relegating women to the status of 'nurses' and 'helpers'.

Gender stereotypes presenting the woman as a hostage to her own reproductive capabilities are tenacious in the hold that they still exert. Cystitus, PMS and menopausal symptoms have been dismissed by male doctors as **pseudo illnesses**. **Porter** (1990) investigated the dismissal of 'women's complaints' by doctors in a clinic in Aberdeen as neurotic, unreasonable or psychogenic – in other words imagined.

Medicine does not exist in a social vacuum. Many of its findings claim the objectivity of science but may well be created to conform to social stereotypes of female fragility and frailness. Women's illnesses are then dismissed by male practitioners as unimportant or dealt with in a way that confirms the woman's lack of control over her own health.

Graham and **Oakley** (1981) see the medicalisation of childbirth as distancing the woman from the experience and reducing it to an event that fits the timetable requirements of the hospital, rather than the emotional needs of the woman. Indeed, babies are often induced to free up the hospital bed, rather than to help the mother.

Martin (1989) suggests that this process of medicalisation has encouraged women to see their bodies as things that need to be controlled, resulting in the almost permanent dieting experiencing of many women, and the increased incidence of anorexia and other eating disorders amongst women.

In addition, medicine increases the risk of iatrogenic problems (disease caused by medical intention) for women. The contraceptive pill carries the risk of thrombosis and a greater chance of cardio vascular disease for those over 40. Hysterectomies and post-menopausal oestrogens in hormone replacement therapies carry with them possible health problems. **Nettleton** (1995) sees the control of reproductive technologies as a tool in establishing medical regulation of the female body.

Study point

Critically examine the contribution that feminists have made to an understanding of gender and health.

Cross Cultural Issues

There is a cultural dimension to the gender and health issue, as there is a relationship between health and social factors. In less developed countries, female life expectancy is higher than that for men, but women are more likely to suffer from malnourishment and to have less access to health care. Only in very poor countries such as Nepal and Bangladesh do men live longer. Female morbidity rates, however, suggest that women are disadvantaged in health in a global way. In Britain, there are clear differences between male and female patterns of health. However, these are even more pronounced when the experiences of women from the developed and developing countries are examined.

Doyal suggests that this demonstrates the weakness of the bio-medical model. The causes of women's ill health in these countries lie in the impact that relative deprivation and poverty has on them, rather than on any biological or medical differences that exist between the genders. This argument is given greater credibility by the health experiences of women in Britain, when the impact of social change in the past 30 years is considered.

SOCIAL CHANGE AND HEALTH

Higher male mortality is due to the dangers inherent in many (male) manual occupations and the risk-taking that is part of male cultural values. Previously, the lower female mortality rate resulted from female exclusion from the workforce and from social conventions associated with behaviour appropriate for females. Women today are far more likely to challenge these stereotypes, both at home and at work, and it is highly likely that the mortality patterns of women will compare with those of men as the lifestyles of the two genders grow more similar. However, the class dimension should not be overlooked as men in Social Class I still have a lower overall mortality rate than women in Social Class V.

Consequently, the emphasis in health has shifted from the bio-medical model, which has stressed intervention and cure based on the biological and medical differences between men and women, in favour of a socio-environmental model, which emphasises prevention and care. In this context factors such as risk assessment of unhealthy practices, vigilance and rational choices are stressed and this has produced a renewed interest in men's health. Male-only diseases such as testicular cancer and prostate cancer have taken succour from the apparent success of screening techniques in improving women's well-being. The implication for both men and women is that, as far as health is concerned, no one should be a prisoner of gender.

Activity

Collect a range of health magazines – some aimed at men, some aimed at women – and compare and contrast the features that they contain and the approaches that they adopt.

HEALTH AND ETHNICITY

The Problem of Definition

A key difficulty that is encountered when examining the impact of ethnicity on health is derived from the problem of defining ethnic origin. For sociologists, the major difficulty is one of establishing terms and the difficulty of doing this makes any study of health and ethnicity problematic.

Ethnicity involves an important question of identity and sociologists have employed a wide range of terms when studying this vexed question. These include 'race', 'ethnicity', specific cultural identities – Greek and Punjabi for example – or even the preferred terms of the groups themselves. For example, the use of the term 'black' for people of Afro Caribbean descent.

'Race' is a social construct lacking any scientific foundation. Nevertheless, as a concept it is used by individuals, groups, institutions and governments to create and recreate meanings and these are heavily associated with assumptions about ethnicity.

Study point
Examine the sociological definitions of the following terms: • race • ethnicity • black. Would the replacement of these terms by another, politically neutral description, help those described by it to gain more equal treatment?

The Problem of Measuring Health and Ethnicity

If it is not clear what the term 'ethnicity' actually means, there are problems for sociologists who are, effectively, using a flawed definition to understand the health experiences of a particular social group. It is more than just a question of imprecise terminology – there are serious deficiencies in the data about different ethnic groups that makes it difficult to investigate their health.

It is only since the 1991 Census that respondents have been asked to specify their ethnic group. Prior to this, researchers had to use birth and death certificates, which only detail an individual's country of birth. This meant that members of ethnic minorities born in this country would have their country of origin recorded as 'United Kingdom'. Similarly, the ethnic origin of British-born inhabitants would not be recorded on death certificates.

This has created a major problem for sociologists and health professionals who have tried to study the mortality and morbidity rates of British-born ethnic minorities. There are enormous gaps in the information available.

So, can ethnicity and health be studied? The nature of this problem should not be used as an excuse not to investigate the health experience of ethnic minorities.

Indeed, the paucity of research suggests that what has previously constituted 'evidence' should be challenged and the scope of existing knowledge extended. In the meantime, we have little choice but to make use of the data currently available – flawed as it is – to try to make some sense of the health needs and experiences of ethnic minority groups. However, as this data was not often compiled for the purpose of showing ethnicity and health, any conclusions drawn from it should be accompanied by a 'health warning'.

Despite this note of caution, the available evidence suggests marked inequities in the UK in the health patterns of ethnic minority groups, compared to the majority, white population. The problems of conceptualising ethnicity aside, a number of studies have drawn fairly robust conclusions based on the different mortality and morbidity rates of different ethnic groups.

Studies carried out by Whitehead (1987) and **Mares** et al (1987) suggest that members of minority groups die from much the same diseases as do the majority population: cancer and circulatory disorders. This conclusion is supported by **Culley** and **Dyson's** study (1993).

However, significant differences have also been identified:

- Africans and Afro Caribbeans tend to have increased incidence of strokes and hypertension (high blood pressure).
- Afro Caribbeans, Indians, Pakistanis and Bangladeshis are more likely to suffer early death from liver cancer, diabetes and tuberculosis.
- Asians suffer particularly from a higher than average rate of heart disease and osteomalacia (softening of the bones), but a lower rate of deaths from cancer compared to the national UK average.
- Mothers born in the Indian subcontinent have a greater chance of experiencing infant mortality.
- More Asians and Afro Caribbeans are likely to suffer from schizophrenic disorders and experience compulsory detention as a result. Moreover, Afro Caribbeans suffering from this condition are more likely to receive electro convulsive therapy (ECT).
- All ethnic minorities show high mortality rates caused by accidents, poisoning and violence.
- All ethnic groups tend to have a higher rate of stillbirths, perinatal mortalities (dead within one week or stillborn) and neonatal mortalities (dead within the first month).

Table 7: *Causes of death by country of birth*		
COUNTRY OF BIRTH	CAUSE OF DEATH	
Africa	Higher rates:	strokes, high blood pressure, violence and attacks, maternal deaths, tuberculosis
	Lower rates:	bronchitis
Indian Subcontinent	Higher rates:	heart disease, diabetes, violence and attacks, tuberculosis
	Lower rates:	bronchitis, certain cancers
Caribbean	Higher rates:	strokes, high blood pressure, violence and attacks, diabetes, maternal deaths
	Lower rates:	bronchitis

SOURCE: CULLEN AND DYSON (1993), ADAPTED FROM WHITEHEAD (1987).

Activity

Using the table above, identify a cause of death that has a lower than average rate of occurrence for all minority groups specified. Also, identify one cause of death that occurs more than average and is common to all of the minority groups.

Explanations For These Health Problems

The problem remains that these health patterns only tell us about groups originating from the Indian Subcontinent, Africa and the Caribbean. We need to find reasons to explain the differential – and often poorer – health suffered by ethnic minorities in the UK.

Those explanations that have been offered take on board many of the features already explored in the section on class and health (page 00) and they tend to centre on genetic, cultural and material factors.

- *Genetic factors* – some disorders do have a genetic cause and can be linked to ethnic grouping. Haemophilia, the inability of the blood to clot, is a mainly European disorder. One in every 3 to 400 Afro Caribbean's has a statistical likelihood of developing sickle-cell anaemia. People from the Mediterranean, the Middle East and Asia are prone to inheriting the blood disorder, thalassaemia. However, it is debatable whether the genetic argument can be used to explain problems such as heart disease, bronchitis and strokes. These diseases are linked to socio economic factors.

- *Cultural factors* – some health problems can be correlated with certain behaviours of ethnic groups. Areas studied in the investigation of culture and identity are salient: diet, lifestyle, traditions and cultural values can have an impact on health.

  Perinatal mortality is high for Asian mothers and it is often blamed on their low attendance rate at ante-natal classes. However, there is a cultural dimension here. It is important to understand that many Asian women feel intimidated by doctors, and are reluctant to be examined by a man.

  In a similar fashion, the relatively high rate of heart disease suffered by Asians is sometimes attributed to the use of cooking fats such as ghee. Also, the ingestion of high carbohydrate foods are blamed for the high incidence of diabetes and obesity. Here, the difficulties surrounding an examination of health and ethnicity are clearly demonstrated. *The Report on Coronary Heart Disease and Asians in Britain* (1986) by the Coronary Prevention Group discovered that these health problems were not suffered by equivalent groups in the Indian Subcontinent. This suggests that analysis of health issues which focuses on cultural factors alone, ignores other important factors such as poverty and stress. It is, therefore, crucial not to consider culture as an all embracing and defining force, but to examine how it combines with other social characteristics and material conditions.

- *Material factors* – this argument suggests that physical factors override considerations such as genetics and culture. Low social class, poor pay, unemployment and dangerous, hazardous occupations are common features of the lives of many members of ethnic minority groups. The concentration of Asians and Afro Caribbean's in low paid, low status, menial jobs in industries that are potentially damaging to the health may have an effect on the higher mortality and morbidity rates of ethnic groups.

  All three contributing factors have been compounded by the racism experienced by many ethnic groups. Poor housing, overcrowding, low status employment, high unemployment and racially motivated violence have all taken their toll on the health of ethnic minorities.

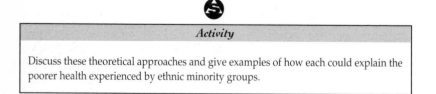

Activity

Discuss these theoretical approaches and give examples of how each could explain the poorer health experienced by ethnic minority groups.

HEALTH, RACE AND IDEOLOGY

McNaught (1987) suggests that racism on both the personal and the institutional level has resulted in ethnic minorities receiving a poor level of care from the NHS. The question about whether the service has marginalised ethnic minorities, both as patients and employees, must be asked. As a provider of health care, the NHS may have failed to change sufficiently to accommodate the variety of cultural and religious beliefs of the increasingly plural culture of the late twentieth century.

Activity
Should the NHS adapt to meet the needs of ethnic minority groups, or should members of minority groups adapt to take advantage of the service that the NHS provides?

OLD AGE AND HEALTH

The study of old age and health is an area of growing interest. Many organisations and university departments have commissioned research into the health of elderly people. An area that has been overlooked for far too long is now being thrown into sharp relief.

DEMOGRAPHIC PROJECTIONS

It is helpful to begin any discussion on health and the health care needs of elderly people by placing the demographic picture in context. Over the period 1991–2031, the Office for Population and Census Studies estimates that the total population of England and Wales will rise by 8 per cent. When this increase is broken down by age, we can see that there are major implications for the health service:

Table 8: *Population increase in different age brackets*	
AGE RANGE	PERCENTAGE INCREASE
45–59	15
60–74	43
75–84	48
85+	138

This contemporary trend is confirmed by a steady rise in the number of elderly people in all Western societies during the twentieth century. In 1900, elderly people constituted about 6 per cent of the population. The number of people aged 65 and over increased to almost 10 per cent by 1931, and again to 15 per cent by 1951. By the 1991 census the number of elderly people had reached 25 per cent of the population. By extrapolation, the number of elderly people looks likely to rise to 27 per cent by 2021.

Study point

Consider the impact that this projected population rise will have on the different care sectors within the health service.

Life expectancy has risen over the past 150 years. In 1841 it was 43 years for women and 41 years for men in Britain. By 1991, this had risen to 80 years for women and 74 years for men. The rise in the number of elderly people is not simply due to the fact that people are living longer. In addition to this rising life expectancy, greater numbers of young people are reaching maturity: the fewer people who die young, the more there are to survive to middle age.

As people live longer, so an increasing proportion of the population requires more care. Demographically, there will be an increasingly large group of people who will have about 20 years of retirement after finishing paid word. However, they will not know whether they will receive treatment if they become ill. Indeed, current research suggests that ageist and prejudicial attitudes are likely to result in their health care needs not being adequately met.

PREJUDICE AND DISCRIMINATION – ANOTHER 'ISM'?

Elderly people are becoming a significant social group with political clout. Sociologists increasingly talk about 'grey power' or the 'greying' or 'rising tide' of the population. However, many elderly people have found the stereotypes of 'useless', 'decayed' and 'decrepit' to be extremely pernicious and hard to escape.

According to **Lehr** old age is a stigmatised identity for most people, with older citizens perceived as ill, retarded, soppy and slow. Indeed, the pejorative and insulting terms that are applied to elderly people would be deemed unacceptable if their equivalents were applied to women or ethnic minorities.

Elderly people are important users of health care in the UK today and, as we have seen, will become more so in the future. The implications of this are only just beginning to be discussed in the available literature and, with this, the possibility that the elderly are suffering inequalities, prejudice and discrimination when it comes to health care provision.

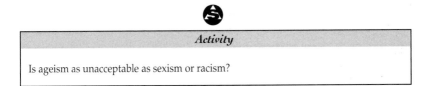

Activity

Is ageism as unacceptable as sexism or racism?

The debate about elderly men and women and health has many strands. Concerns about older people relate to the levels of disease and disability that they suffer and the costs that an increasing number of older people represent for health care providers. Added to this are the decisions being applied by health care professionals, the public at large – and even the elderly themselves – about whether they deserve medical help.

Table 9: *Major causes of mortality in old people*						
Cause of death	AGE: MEN (YEARS)			AGE: WOMEN (YEARS)		
	65–74	75–84	85+	65–74	75–84	85*
Heart disease, stroke	48%	49%	46%	43%	53%	51%
Growths, tumours	33%	25%	17%	35%	21%	11%
Respiratory	9%	13%	20%	9%	10%	16%
Other	9%	13%	18%	13%	17%	21%

SOURCE: OPCS MONITOR DH2 92/2

MAJOR CAUSES OF MORBIDITY IN OLD PEOPLE

The **General Household Survey (GHS)** indicates a number of significant causes of illness in old people:

- cardiovascular or cerebrovascular disease
- osteoarthritis
- osteoporosis
- incontinence
- dementia
- depression.

Table 10: *NHS spending on different services*	
SERVICES	FIGURES (£ MILLIONS)
Maternity	976
Learning disabilities	1,133
Other	1,536
Other community	1,573
Mental illness	2,351
Elderly	2,660
Acute	10,257
Administration	875

Table 11: *NHS spending on different age groups*	
AGE GROUP (YEARS)	FIGURES (£ MILLIONS)
Births	1,147
0–4	1,365
5–15	1,210
16–44	4,757
45–64	3,942
65–74	3,277
75–84	3,600
85+	2,063

SOURCE: *THE NHS HANDBOOK* 1997–98

Activity

Look at the data given in Table 10 and calculate the percentage of spending that goes on the care of the elderly. Compare this with the percentage spent on the 75–85+ age group (see Table 10).

What observations can you make from this?

INEQUALITIES IN HEALTH CARE FOR ELDERLY PEOPLE

- Older people are more than twice as likely as those below the age of 65 to die from heart disease and more than five times as likely to have a heart attack. Despite this, Age Concern has discovered that about 20 per cent of coronary care units (CCUs) operate an age-related admissions policy. A further 40 per cent of CCUs limit the allocation of 'clot busting' drugs to the elderly.
- Most cancer sufferers are elderly but they are treated less than younger sufferers. About 1000 elderly people die each year because doctors judge that their age makes it unlikely that they can cope with surgery, radiotherapy or chemotherapy. Such judgements are often not based on any clinical research – indeed the elderly are often excluded from research trials – but on a socially constructed notion of age.
- 63 per cent of women with breast cancer come from the 65+ age group. Whilst breast screening is an effective way of detecting cancer in this group, women of this age are excluded from the programme of automatic invitations to screenings.
- The older a person is, the less likely it is that they will be treated for lung cancer. Over half of patients with inoperable non-small lung cancer are aged 65 or over. However, palliative chemotherapy, which can alleviate suffering, is usually offered to younger people.
- The possibility of kidney failure rises with age. However, about two-thirds of kidney patients aged 70–79 are rejected for dialysis programmes or transplants. This rejection rate rises to seven-eighths in the 80+ age category. All this, despite clinical evidence showing that older people have a greater survival rate – and a lesser chance of organ rejection – than younger sufferers.

Activity
'Older people are under-researched, under-diagnosed, under-valued, and sometimes over-drugged.' Dr Arup Banerjee, President Elect of the British Geriatric Society (1996).
How far do you agree with this assessment of the health care experience of the elderly?

Economics or Prejudice?

There is a growing tendency amongst health care professionals, purchasers and providers (see Chapter 6) to use age alone as a mechanism for excluding older people from certain types of health care. Investigations by the **Medical Research**

Council and Age Concern have suggested that health service professionals, and the general public, assume that the elderly benefit less from medical and surgical intervention than younger people.

It must be stressed that this contention has yet to be supported by hard evidence. However, if it is true, it is possible that an attitude is being applied which is based on the notion that older people are not as deserving of medical help as younger people, because they offer less to society. Exclusionist policies are being devised that discriminate against people, simply because they are too old, too risky or not worth it. Perhaps it is because the victims of ill health are old and are considered to have 'lasted well' or have had 'a good innings' that such arbitrary criteria are applied in a way that would be unacceptable if the recipients were women or members of ethnic minority groups.

Whilst resources play a part in this process, the denial of access to heart treatment, cancer services and renal treatment by clinicians is also due to the use of chronological age being used as a measure of biological fitness. At the end of the twentieth century it appears as if older people experience discrimination across the board in health care, from acute care to rehabilitation services, from preventative programmes to primary care.

Consequently, there is now a growing concern surrounding inequalities in health care provision for elderly people. So far, this chapter has considered inequality mainly in the context of differences between different social groups. It is also important to recognise and investigate inequalities in provision during the different stages of an individual's life.

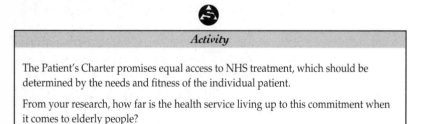

Activity
The Patient's Charter promises equal access to NHS treatment, which should be determined by the needs and fitness of the individual patient.
From your research, how far is the health service living up to this commitment when it comes to elderly people?

The Challenge for the Next Century

Research that examines the differences in access to the NHS according to age is urgently needed. Much of the available research concentrates on younger age groups and has been dominated by class, and to a lesser extent, gender and ethnicity. In particular, research is lacking which examines the impact of these social characteristics on an individual beyond the age of retirement.

SUMMARY

Modern sociology has been concerned with the importance of class and the impact that it has upon our lives. This is true of many of the investigations into the social patterning of health. However, it is important to consider the other social characteristics that people possess and how these may contribute towards their health care experience.

Group work

Draw up a chart illustrating the main social characteristics that affect health. For each one, itemise the key explanations which attempt to account for differential health experiences.

Coursework

Investigate the population and health care needs in your local area. Carry out research to establish whether the population is changing with respect to age, ethnic mix, class and gender. Consider the demands that any changes may have upon the health care providers. Research the health care experiences of the local population and support this with an investigation into the role of health care professionals in identifying need and providing treatment.

Exam Hints

'Identify and evaluate different sociological explanations of the maintenance of social class inequalities in health and health care.'

A possible answer to this question will begin by examining the issues concerning the distribution of health and illness by social class, using the classic research from the Whitehead and Black Reports. The answer should indicate that class is only one source of inequality and mention – *but not explore* – the issues concerning gender, ethnicity and age. Then go on to consider artefact, social selection, cultural and structural explanations. Conclude by giving an overview of the strengths and weaknesses of each position and indicate that some are more useful than others.

1 'The social patterns of ill health closely reflect the distribution of income and wealth.' Discuss.
2 Critically evaluate the relationship between class and social background, and the extent and distribution of different types of illness.
3 Outline and evaluate different sociological accounts of the continuation of gender inequalities in health care.
4 'Artefact explanations of health inequalities suggest that the apparent health differences between social groups result from the difficulties in measuring a complex issue such as health.' Critically consider sociological arguments for and against this view.

5

MENTAL ILLNESS AND DISABILITY

Introduction

EACH CHAPTER WILL examine the position of mentally ill people within our society. It will indicate that those with mental illness are often treated unequally by the medical profession itself, as well as within society. This chapter will examine the historical development of the concept of mental health and establish links between this and the sociological perspectives concerned. It will then go on to consider present policies such as 'return to the community'.

The key issues that will be explored will focus on three key areas:

- Defining mental health and disability.
- The historical development of mental illness.
- Research and present trends.

DEFINING MENTAL HEALTH AND DISABILITY

The area of mental illness is still one that is enshrouded with fear, prejudice and misunderstanding. Firstly, it is important to distinguish between mental illness and mental, or learning, disability. Mental illnesses are conditions such as depression, anxiety, eating disorders and schizophrenia, whereas learning disabilities are specific difficulties found in children of normal or above average intelligence such as dyslexia. Secondly, it is important to acknowledge that mental illness is not related to intelligence. Thirdly, it is necessary to recognise how many people suffer from mental disorders. Schizophrenia, for instance, a serious psychotic disorder has an incidence of 0.2 to 2 per cent, according to different studies throughout the world. Anorexia Nervosa has a prevalence of

Table 12: *Theorists, concepts and issues in this chapter*			
KEY THEORIST	THEORY	KEY CONCEPTS	KEY ISSUES
Szasz	Interactionist	'Mad' label is applied to people we do not like or agree with	• Challenge to bio-medical model
Goffmann	Interactionist	Process of 'mortification of the self'	• The psychiatric hospital creates its own sub-culture
Rosenhan	Interactionist	The medical system reinforces 'mentally ill labels'	• Challenge to institutional treatment
Foucault	Post-structuralist	Mental illness is a relative concept	• Mental institutions are just a phase in the historical development of mental disorders

0.5 to 1 per cent of adolescent females, usually in Western societies; Bulimia affects 1 to 3 per cent of adolescent females. According to a 1994 survey in the UK of 10,000 adults, 1500 people who had been in psychiatric care and 1100 homeless people, one in seven adults experience depression, anxiety or some other kind of psychiatric problem. These latter could be eating disorders, phobias, panic attacks, Post-Traumatic Shock Disorder (PTSD), Generalised Anxiety Disorder (GAD) or Seasonal Affective Disorder (SAD).

It is essential, therefore, to realise that mental illnesses range from anxiety and mild depression through personality and conduct disorders to severe neurotic or psychotic disorders. Most of us will experience one or more of these disorders throughout our lives. In fact, many famous people such as Diogenes, Winston Churchill, Van Gogh, Virginia Wolf, Keats, Abraham Lincoln, Handel, Spike Milligan and action theorist Max Weber to name but a few, have achieved outstanding success despite suffering recurring mental illness.

Activity
Consider definitions for the following words and add them to your vocabulary list:

- neurotic
- phobia
- dyslexia
- psychotic
- somatic

- paraplegic
- schizophrenia
- autism
- trepanning.

Mental ill health has often been the area of illness most stigmatised and misunderstood, perhaps because it is less clearly or obviously linked with a germ or obvious biological disorder. Consequently, **Szasz** (1974) points out people often call others 'mad' when they do not like them or if they disagree with them. In this way the label 'mad' has been used as a method of social and often political control. We have already mentioned the labels applied to slaves in America and dissidents in the former USSR. Women too have been labelled in this way. In our society, they have been called 'abnormal' for not wishing to have children, or for having them out of wedlock. This could only happen, argue feminists, in a patriarchal society that sees women only as mothers and wives.

Mental illness can, therefore, be defined as any disorder affecting the behaviour and personality of an individual so as to prevent them functioning adequately within their society. This in turn lends itself to all sorts of interpretations by others in society. In psychological terms the **DSM** and **ICD** classification systems give more precise advice on the diagnosis of abnormality.

DSM AND ICD

The ICD is the major classification system – **The International Classification of Diseases** – published by the World Health Organisation (WHO). The DSM is published by the American Psychiatric Association and stands for **Diagnostic and Statistical Manual of Mental Disorders**. The DSM (tenth edition) states the definition of mental health as follows:

> *In DSM-IV, each of the mental disorders is conceptualized as a clinically significant behavioural or psychological syndrome or pattern that occurs in an individual and that is associated with present distress (e.g. a painful symptom) or disability (i.e. impairment in one or more important areas of functioning) or with a significantly increased risk of suffering death, pain, disability or an important loss of freedom. In addition, this syndrome or pattern must not be merely an expectable and culturally sanctioned response to a particular event, for example the death of a loved one. Whatever its original cause, it must currently be considered a manifestation of a behavioural, psychological or biological dysfunction in the individual. Neither deviant behaviour (e.g. political, religious or sexual) nor conflicts that are primarily between the individual and society are mental disorders unless the deviance or conflict is a symptom of a dysfunction in the individual, as described above.*

Study point

Consider the above quote. What term does the DSM use instead of 'abnormal' in the definition of mental disorder? Why do you think this is? Where can you find evidence of political, religious or sexual behaviour being labelled 'deviant' and/or a mental disorder?

'NORMAL' AND 'ABNORMAL' IDENTITIES

If, as **Erving Goffman** (1969, 1970) suggests, we manage our identities and present them in everyday life, then being 'normal' is crucial. Many people work hard at presenting themselves as normal. In fact, to a certain extent, everyone has to work hard to do this, whatever their sphere of life or profession. An electrician coming into our homes to repair a broken appliance is expected to have up-to-date knowledge of electricity and to wear the appropriate clothes or uniform. A sociology lecturer is likewise expected to know more than the students, to quote research and reading lists and to dress as a sociology lecturer should! Certain standards of behaviour are also expected – the electrician should not help him or herself to food in the refrigerator and the lecturer should not abuse the students.

There are individuals who have disabilities and for these people there may be a contradiction between *virtual social identity* (how they see themselves) and *actual social identity* (how others see them), leading to a 'spoiled' identity.

In our society people tend to see only a person's disability. This becomes the dominant label. Thus, the disability influences everything they do. In this case, their presentation of 'self' is a problem. They may *try* to appear as 'normal' as possible, hiding their disability and thus affect **normalisation**. Otherwise, they may use resistance, not by hiding the disability, but by using it to form a community of disabled. **Tom Shakespeare** (1998) has pointed out that disablement is created by societies that fail to cater for those who do not meet with that society's ideas of what is 'normal'. Society *makes* people disabled by failing to build environments in which wheelchairs can move about easily, for example. **Steve Taylor** points out (1994), that blindness is a striking example of the ways in which societal action can 'shape people's experience of a disabling condition'. He refers to **Scott's** classic study (1969) which examines the psychological theory that blindness produces certain personality characteristics such as passivity and compliance. From his study based in the USA, Scott provides a different explanation. He argues that emphasis is placed on the problems of the blind person's psychological adjustment to loss of sight and the product of this adjustment in the blind person's personality. The personality is therefore the product of the socialisation process. The blind person comes to accept the experts' view of who they are. In societies (such as Sweden) where blindness is seen as more of a technical handicap, rather than a loss, blind people are more integrated and there is less talk of the blind person's personality. In fact, Steve Taylor points out that international studies indicate the importance of society's reaction to conditions such as epilepsy, physical disability and being HIV positive.

Activity

See if you can borrow a wheelchair and, together with a helper, see what it is like to go shopping or to travel by public transport. Choose an area where you are not well known. Do people treat you or speak to you differently? Your college may have a wheel chair for first aid purposes. Alternatively, the Red Cross, or a similar organisation, may be able to help you.

POINTS OF EVALUATION

1 Mental illness and disability are obviously, at least partly, socially constructed.
2 Mental illness encompasses a whole range of disorders, from mild depression to schizophrenia. Disability can range from being short sighted to being severely physically disabled.
3 Over time, we view these disorders differently. Thus, now we can correct short sightedness with spectacles and we no longer label homosexuality as a mental illness. (In 1980 it was dropped from the DSM classification of mental illness.)
4 Therefore, the concepts of mental illness and disability are ever changing, according to our state of knowledge, prevailing attitudes and technological advances that help with coping strategies.

THE HISTORICAL DEVELOPMENT OF MENTAL ILLNESS

It was Szasz (1974) who was one of the first to challenge the biomedical model of mental illness. Szasz argued that mental illness was discovered in the mid-nineteenth century, when behaviour or bodily function was added to the study of bodily structure as the subject matter of medicine. People who complained of feeling ill when the seemed fit could not be suffering from a functional illness. Szasz's conclusions were that:

- strictly speaking, disease can only affect the body and not the mind
- psychiatric diagnoses are stigmatising labels, phrased to resemble medical diagnoses and applied to people whose behaviour annoys or offends others
- mental illness is not really something a person has, but something he does or is and, therefore, it cannot be subject to treatment or cure, but might be changed
- the prestige and power of psychiatrists has been inflated by more and more phenomena which are defined as within the scope of their discipline.

Szasz's work is certainly important because it makes us question what are now taken-for-granted assumptions about 'abnormal' behaviour, and it makes us focus on the psychiatrist as an official involved in the labelling process. It also makes us question what we take to be 'abnormal' behaviour, and helps us to focus on the real personal and social problems people living in society face. On the other hand, there is a danger of overstating the case and making us feel that nothing could or should be done to mould the behaviour of people committing anti-social acts. There are certainly many psychiatrists who would argue that Szasz is misrepresenting their profession.

Foucault

Michael Foucault's historical perspective demonstrates that mental illness and the 'treatments' prescribed depend as much upon social factors as biological ones. For Foucault, the study of history involves working out how and why different discourses came to be established. This is essentially a study of power. Power, according to Foucault, is exercised in two ways:

1 in order that a discourse will come into being
2 power is exercised *by* a discourse so that it determines what people think and know and, therefore, how they behave.

Foucault became well known for his accounts of the history of medicine, madness, sexuality, punishment and the body. For him, the emergence of the idea of madness as illness is a good example of the rise to dominance of a discourse. Foucault argued that up until the mid-eighteenth century, mental illness was regarded as a result of possession by evil forces. In medieval times, he claims, sanity and madness were intermingled. Madness was often associated with holiness, wisdom, even genius. Hence, there were court jesters who were allowed to ridicule the establishment and who are often shown as being the real 'wise' men in many of Shakespeare's plays.

However, **Porter** (1986) disagrees and sees this as a hopelessly romanticised view. He makes the point that the mad were not integrated into society, but were ostracised and ridiculed (see again Shakespeare's treatment of Malvolio in *Twelfth Night* and King Lear, himself). Lower class 'lunatics' faired even worse. However, Foucault insists that incarceration in 'mad houses' was relatively rare, well into the eighteenth century.

The treatment for mental illness may go back to Neolithic times: skulls have been found with **trepanned** holes. These were, perhaps, the first attempts at physically rectifying mental problems. However, it is not until much later that we hear of horrific physical treatments for mental illness, such as bleeding, vomiting, high speed rotation, cold baths and insulin coma therapy. From being associated in the seventeenth and eighteenth centuries with over indulgence or moral weakness (such views still linger on), in the twentieth century the cause of mental illness was said to be physical malfunction or psychological disturbance in childhood.

The Enlightenment facilitated the interpretation of 'mad' as being 'without reason', characterised as the period was by the rise in rationality, reason and science. In Medieval Europe the eradication of leprosy left buildings used for isolation of lepers empty. This, according to Foucault, provided possibilities for the exclusion from 'normal' society of other categories of people, particularly the insane. The creation of asylums made the discipline of psychiatry possible. Thus, grew the profession and a new medical discourse allowed the social control of those whose behaviour was deemed to be disturbing to others – social control via hospitalisation.

In the twentieth century mental illness became medicalised and treatable according to the bio-medical model. This period saw the rise of surgery, such as lobotomy; Electro Convulsive Therapy (ECT); drug therapy and psychotherapy.

Psychosurgery is now only used as a last resort and the effectiveness of ECT is being questioned in many countries. It is considered inhumane, especially as how it actually works is not fully understood. As we move into the twenty-first century there are many psychiatric schools of thought and not just one model of mental illness. Nowadays a combination of treatments is often preferred: short-term drug therapy plus psychotherapy to sort out the underlying problems, for example.

More recently there has been a change in attitude to institutional treatment of mental illness, which will be considered in the next section.

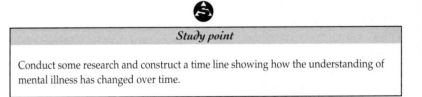

Study point

Conduct some research and construct a time line showing how the understanding of mental illness has changed over time.

RESEARCH AND PRESENT TRENDS

Some sociologists have challenged the traditional view that an institution is the best place to treat the mentally ill. One of these is Erving Goffman (1968), who claims that psychiatric hospitals create their own subculture. As an interactionist he claims that mentally ill people do not get cured in hospital, rather they learn to 'act mad' and this reduces any chance of returning to the outside world. Goffman outlines the phrases that those labelled 'sick' go through as:

1 *The process of mortification of the self* – the phase in which the patient's identify is removed and their name is replaced with numbers, strip searching, ritual ablution, lack of privacy etc.

2 *Learning a new role* – this phase involves learning the new role. Those who comply are rewarded with privileges and those who don't are punished by such things as isolation, drugs, ECT or surgery.

3 *Responding to the label 'mentally ill'* – the way in which a patient responds can be by:
   - *withdrawal* or *introversion*, which is seen as part of the illness
   - *rebellion*, which is also seen as part of the illness
   - *institutionalisation* in which the patient accepts that they are mentally ill and feels safer in the hospital
   - an alternative response is *conversion*: the patient accepts their new role and now tows to the staff
   - finally, the patient might 'play it cool'. This, according to Goffman, is the most common response and is one of the ways to limit damage to the self by the institution. This is the response where the patient keeps his or her head down.

Overall, Goffman points to the fact that behaviour learnt or expressed within the institution reduces the chance of being released. In his classic interactionist study of hoarding behaviour amongst mental patients in asylums (1968) he records how patients collected all sorts of apparently useless and trivial objects, such as pieces of string and toilet paper. For the staff, this behaviour confirms the label attached to the patient. It is evidence of deep-seated anxieties and insecurities. However, Goffman argues that it is logical behaviour, because inside the institution these items are difficult to come by and lack of privacy means they have to guard them closely.

Edwin Lement's equally famous account (1967) of the social construction of paranoia also demonstrates the aspects of labelling that are magnified within the confines of an institution. Paranoia is when the sufferer imagines he or she is being watched. However, once this condition is diagnosed, the feared conspiracy actually does happen. The 'ill' person *is* secretly observed! For the labellers of such people (ie, the psychiatric staff), an acknowledgement of the need for treatment is the first step to a cure. The fact that this might simply be the last stage in the social construction of a mental condition which may have begun with an initial labelling by others is, of course, not considered.

Rosenhan's ethnomethodological experiment in 1975 was concerned with how people come to be defined as insane. Research volunteers claimed that they had heard voices and sought medical help. They were admitted to 12 different hospitals where they stopped pretending and behaved normally. None of the volunteers were recognised as fakes. All were diagnosed as schizophrenic and all were discharged with the illness being in 'remission'. Rosenhan then made an even more serious challenge to the bio-medical model and institutionalisation in particular when he reversed the experiment and told hospital staff to *expect* people to try to gain entrance by faking illness. In the following three months 41 out of 193 cases were identified by staff as being suspicious – all were genuinely seeking help.

Of course, there were ethical problems with Rosenhan's experiment. In addition, there are criticisms of Lement and Goffman, that their research is too small scale to generalise from and that they rely on individual interpretation. However, studies like these have drawn attention to processes of diagnosis and institutionalisation.

Like other illnesses, **Trowler** (1996) has demonstrated that mental illness is socially distributed and this further challenges the bio-medical model. More women than men are likely to die while suffering from mental disorders, although this may also be linked to the fact that women live longer. Also, working class mothers seem to be more prone to depression than middle class mothers. Black patients seem more likely to be admitted to mental hospitals than white patients with similar symptoms. There is an increase in suicide and depression amongst young unemployed males. More and more the link between mental disorders and social conditions is made manifest. Afro Caribbeans and Asians are more like to be diagnosed as schizophrenic and placed in mental institutions (Trowler, 1996). This evidence must be seen alongside evidence that suggests ethnic minorities are more likely to suffer high rates of unemployment. **Graham Scambler** (1991) has pointed out that contact with psychiatric services may be seen as stigmatising. So much so that much mental illness may be contained within the family. In fact, fear of a psychiatric hospital admission may even inhibit contact with a general practitioner.

Community Care
Partly as a reaction to evidence such as this, the end of the twentieth century has seen a growing belief that ill people are as much a part of society as the healthy and should be fully integrated. We have seen modern town planning incorporating access for the disabled. We have also seen a move towards a 'return to the community' or 'return to the family' policy. This has been viewed as a money saving policy with the aim of reducing public taxation and public expenditure, and returning responsibility to individuals and families. As a consequence, many institutions have been closed, there has been a reduction in the number of beds and the development of care provision within the community. This 'return to the community' program is primarily associated with the New Right and in particular the Conservative Governments of the late 1980s and 1990s. Each person being discharged is given a care plan, a professional 'key worker' and/or access to medical or social work teams. The idea is to support the individual to live alone or with their family, alongside clinical monitoring in case they should need further hospitalisation.

These principles have great support both medically and politically. However, the actual practical implementation has suffered considerable criticism. There has been a general attempt to **normalise** people with a range of mental health problems. This normalisation includes the promotion of positive role models, practical training for people with learning difficulties and counselling.

Community care has three basic characteristics:

1   It takes place outside any institution.
2   Individuals are treated as normal members of the community.
3   Support comes mainly from lay carers – especially family – supported by health and welfare workers

Study point
Conduct a formal debate with two speakers, (one for the motion, one against) seconds and a chairperson. The motion: 'Mental illness is not an objective fact.' Take a vote at the end.

POINTS OF EVALUATION

The advantages of community care

1   Community care is intellectually satisfying: it is more humane. The mentally ill have been separated from the rest of society for too long – most do not pose a risk to the public and there is a growing belief that modern society is becoming increasingly unreal in that it marginalises too many groups, including the mentally ill (Chapter 3). This idea is similar to Anthony Giddens' 'personal meaninglessness' concept in which he says we are unprepared by modern life for issues such as sickness and death, which are hidden away so that we do not have to think about them.
2   Community care is cheaper than institutional care and the savings can be spent on more effective health care.
3   It avoids the institutionalisation (as demonstrated by Lement, Rosenhan and Goffman) which prevents return to the world outside the institution.
4   Community care is now practically possible given that drug therapy is more effective and long lasting.

The disadvantages of community care

1   Even in 1979 **Scull** pointed out that some people who 'return to the community' might not be safe for themselves or for others. This has led to suicides, to some ex-patients putting themselves and others at risk and to a few cases in which members of the public have been killed by ex-patients.
2   Return to the community might be effective if we had a caring community and if support carers were efficiently and properly trained. However, it is argued

that care in the community has not been properly organised or funded. Many ex-patients are isolated, many families struggle to support mentally ill members and many communities campaign against the siting of houses for mentally ill people in their area.

3   in some areas institutions were run down too quickly and, as a consequence, insufficient community care was set up. This has led to problems of inefficient communication.

4   Because so many beds were lost, patients were returned to the community too soon. This has led to the 'revolving door' situation: re-admittance, discharge, re-admittance, discharge and so on.

5   The community care program has been more about cost cutting than improving the lot of mentally ill people. This has led to points 3 and 4 above, as well as the poor training of some professional workers and their low pay.

6   Many ex-patients find themselves in poor housing conditions or even homeless. Private care homes have increased. But these are often unregulated and some have been accused of abuse and neglect of patients.

As previously stated, the 'return to the community' program has been supported by rightwing and leftwing politicians, but there is a recognition that it may have proceeded with too much haste. The 1997 Labour Government, led by Tony Blair, has pledged to provide secure institutions for more severely disturbed mentally

CARE IN THE COMMUNITY, IF PROPERLY FUNDED AND SUPPORTED, MAY BE A MORE HUMANE WAY OF LOOKING AFTER PEOPLE WHO ARE MENTALLY ILL. HOWEVER, IT IS ARGUED THAT THE SCHEME HAS BEEN A FAILURE DUE TO A LACK OF FINANCIAL AND ORGANISATIONAL AID, AND FOLLOWING THE HARM CAUSED BY SUFFERERS TO THEMSELVES AND OTHERS.

ill people. In particular, this is a response to pressure applied by organisations such as The Zito Trust, which have campaigned following murders committed by ex-patients.

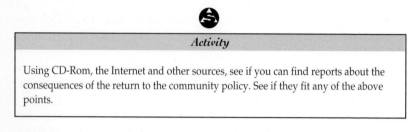

Activity

Using CD-Rom, the Internet and other sources, see if you can find reports about the consequences of the return to the community policy. See if they fit any of the above points.

SUMMARY

Mental health has often been seen as separate to other health issues, the move towards community care may be seen as an indication that at last it may be coming in from the cold.

Group work

Create a role play based around a diagnosed, mentally ill person and how they are interpreted by different people at different times. This will require research into the symptoms of the particular mental illness that you have chosen to depict. Then, in turns, present your situation to the rest of the class. You could choose people or characters from history or literature, for instance, Karl Marx, Foucault, a medieval monk, a seventeenth-century puritan or a nineteenth-century doctor.

Exam Hints

'Assess the contribution of sociology to an understanding of mental illness.'

This essay could start with an acknowledgement of the understanding of mental illness before a sociological interpretation existed. It should, therefore, consider the rise of science, psychology, as well as sociology, and how these also contributed to our knowledge. The essay could then go on to consider particular sociologist's contributions to the social nature of mental illness: Goffman,

Foucault, and Szasz should be covered. You may also include Rosenhan, Lement and others.

The essay should conclude with a consideration of the change in the care of and attitudes towards mentally ill people, which have come about, at least partly, from sociological research.

Practice questions

1 'Mental illness is not an objective fact, but is primarily a social and political construction.' Discuss.
2 'Psychiatrists have the power to label a person mentally ill.' Examine the implications of this statement for an understanding of the nature of mental illness.

Coursework

1 Conduct a survey, including an attitude survey, into the success or otherwise of the 'return to the community' policy. (If possible, interview local authorities, social service departments, volunteer workers and welfare campaigners.)
2 Investigate the social composition of those who are carers. What do they do; how much support do they receive; how many are women?
3 Conduct a survey into attitudes to mental health or disability. Are certain types of mental illness or disability stigmatised? Are people blamed in any way for their disabilities?

6

THE CHANGING PROVISION OF HEALTH CARE

Introduction

THE NATIONAL HEALTH service (NHS) affects most of the population of the UK. Most people have been treated by the NHS or expect to use the service at some time. Even those who pay for their own health insurance could use the NHS in an emergency. The service has an important social and political dimension. There is widespread and strong conviction for a publicly owned and funded health service that is comprehensive, open to all and free at the point of delivery.

However, despite this public support the NHS is widely perceived as being in a state of crisis. The high expectations that people have about the quality and availability of health care have resulted in enormous pressures on the system. It is important, therefore, to investigate the NHS as a political issue and to view it in the context of the battles that have taken place between the two main political parties over the past 20 years.

This chapter will explore this theme and will begin by briefly discussing the background to the creation of the NHS. Then it will focus on four important themes:

- The creation of the NHS in 1948.
- The political consensus concerning health between 1950 and 1970.
- The New Right challenge to this challenge to this consensus after 1979.
- The intention of the New Labour Government elected in 1997.

Table 13: *Key developments in the extension of health care provision in the UK*		
EVENT	DATE	RESULT
Poor Law Act	1601	Local parishes to provide poor relief paid for out of the local rates
Poor Law Amendment Act	1834	Poor Law infirmaries established
Public Health Acts	1848 1875	To prevent water contamination, local health authorities charged with taking responsibility for health
National Insurance Scheme	1911	Provided a limited health insurance for most workers
Beveridge Report	1942	Aimed to abolish the 'five giant evils'
Postwar health consensus	1950 to 1970	Both Labour and Conservative governments agreed over the principle of a National Health Service provided for by the government
The New Right reforms	1979 to 1997	The Conservative challenge to the politics of consensus sees a policy of market liberalism introduced into the NHS
The New Labour Government	1997	Proposals put forward to take the NHS into the next millennium

HEALTH, POLITICS AND POWER

Medicine is more than the application of great scientific discoveries. It is also about **power** and **power relationships**. Any study of medicine and health should acknowledge the surrounding structural, historical, political, social and economic context, if the impact that medicine has is to be fully appreciated.

As you read about the steps that Britain took towards the creation of a system of widespread medical treatment, consider whether the desire to help people was also driven by the need to *control* them. It can be argued that a further function of the Poor Law infirmaries, asylums and hospitals of the nineteenth century was to control people who were poor, old, mentally and physically ill. Doctors became more organised and more powerful as the bio-medical view of ill health began to emerge and to exercise control over people.

Study point

Refer back to Chapter 3 and consider ways in which the bio-medical model of health has resulted in medicine acting as a form of social control.

BACKGROUND TO THE CREATION OF THE NHS

From the second half of the nineteenth century and throughout the first 50 years of the twentieth century, there was a steady move towards government acceptance of responsibility for the health and welfare of its citizens.

The early nineteenth century was characterised by a *laissez faire* approach by governments who saw no need to intervene in the lives of its citizenry, believing that economic market forces would do more to benefit the lives of people than statutes and legislation ever could.

Gradually – and reluctantly – governments were forced to accept that they had a duty and a responsibility to regulate the lives of their populations. One of the first, hesitant, steps towards governmental acceptance of its obligation to provide help for the health of the population came with the **1834 Poor Law Amendment Act**. This obliged the workhouses that were created to house and a employ poor people and to establish sick wards. However, the harsh penal regime that characterised the workhouses sought to punish the 'undeserving' poor. There was, as yet, no benign attempt to improve the health of the poor and the sick. Rather, treatment aimed to punish them for getting into their situation.

The appaling health of the nation continued and this led to the creation of a **General Board of Health** in 1848. The Board assumed responsibility for the Poor Law infirmaries. As a piece of legislation, it established little of any practical use, but it is a landmark in that it represented a recognition that government had a *duty* to improve the health of the general public.

At the turn of the century, Britain's imperial pride was dented by the fact that many men were deemed medically unfit to serve for military duty during the Boer War. Also, with more and more working men now able to vote, successive governments began to give even more serious consideration to issues such as health, welfare and education for the working class.

In an immense power struggle with the House of Lords in 1909 over the so-called 'people's budget' the Liberal Government introduced plans for a **National Insurance**. Contributions from employers and workers would go towards the establishment of a limited framework that would provide pensions and other welfare benefits. An embryonic welfare state was to grow from this.

After the First World War, the State began assuming even more responsibility for health. The **Ministry of Health** was set up in 1919 and by 1929 the Poor Law infirmaries became the responsibility of local authorities: municipal hospitals were the result.

The Second World War prompted even more change, with the Government assuming full control of both voluntary and municipal hospitals as part of the **Emergency Medical Service** created in 1939. Indeed the very experience of total war, in which people suffered equally irrespective of their social class, was to contribute to the creation of the collectivist, egalitarian notions that characterised the immediate postwar period.

Gradually, the State began absorbing many of the agencies that had developed to deal with social support in the informal sector, the voluntary sector and the private sector.

- *The informal sector* – before the State accepted responsibility for public health, most people would have relied on this sector, namely family, friends and neighbours.
- *The voluntary sector* – voluntary agencies, charities and religious movements provided a patchy system of health care for those who could not afford to pay.
- *The private sector* – before the creation of the NHS in 1948, any health care not provided by the informal and the voluntary sector would have been private. Health was determined by the ability of an individual to pay.

Activity

Consider the likely scenario for an unemployed person suffering from a heart complaint before the creation of the NHS. What health care avenues would be available?

THE NATIONAL HEALTH SERVICE

We have seen how ongoing historical developments gradually lead to the creation of a National Health Service in Britain. The Second World War had created a general determination that Britain would rebuild itself and that this new Britain would be better than the one that had gone before.

With hindsight, *The Beveridge Report* of 1942 can be seen to represent a sea change in government thinking about health and welfare. This document helped to shape both the attitudes and the legislation of the immediate postwar period.

This report on 'Social Insurance and Allied Services' provided the blueprint for many of the changes introduced by the Labour administration of 1945–51. During this period the foundations for a welfare state were laid; it was to be regarded as desirable by both the Labour and Conservative parties over the next 20 years (the postwar consensus).

THE 'FIVE GIANT SOCIAL EVILS'

The Beveridge Report identified five major areas of concern that needed to be tackled. These were:

- want
- disease
- ignorance
- squalor
- idleness.

The **National Health Act** of 1948 promised to help in the concerted fight against these evils and aimed to create a system of universal health care, free at the point of delivery. In the postwar spirit of renewal this idea received widespread support from the public, but also considerable opposition from some politicians who were alarmed at the potential expense of the experiment.

Activity

Why were conditions right in the Britain of 1945 for the creation of a welfare state?

A great deal of opposition also came from doctors, who were reluctant to shift from private practice to State employment. Indeed, the strength of their resistance forced the Minister of Health at the time, **Aneurin Bevin**, to allow doctors to enjoy dual status as independent contractors paid to work for the State and also able to practice privately. Thus from the outset, Britain never really had a State run health service. However, a corollary of this is the fact that it was only *because* of the continuation of private practice that the NHS was able to continue. The revenue generated from private practice propped up the ailing service for many years.

The NHS was founded on a tripartite arrangement of GPs, local health authorities and regional health authorities. From the very outset, the service was plagued with bureaucratic and structural problems. This resulted in the universal and collective aims of the welfare state being undermined by the professional autonomy exercised by doctors and hospitals. A sort of 'gentleman's agreement' developed in which it was assumed that the medical profession would make spending decisions based solely on their medical expertise and sense of professional ethics. Doctors, acting neutrally and logically, would deliver policies that would improve the health of the nation, it was believed.

Essentially, the structure created in 1948 changed little until 1974. Indeed, a considerable degree of consensus was demonstrated by successive Labour and

Conservative governments regarding the health service in this period. Both parties shared a commitment to the ideological notions of a welfare state. Moreover, in the climate of sustained economic growth that characterised this period it was widely believed in government circles that the welfare state was triumphant and that the ideals of the Beveridge Report had been achieved.

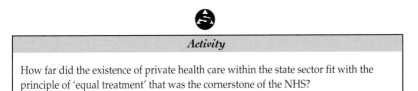

Activity

How far did the existence of private health care within the state sector fit with the principle of 'equal treatment' that was the cornerstone of the NHS?

Whilst initially a definite consensus existed between the two main political parties, cracks began to emerge because of the spiralling costs of the service. These rose from £437 million in 1949 to £27,000 million in 1990. Well before this latter figure had been reached, the Labour and Conservative parties had begun to take a very different stance on the health service.

The commitment to the principle of the universality of welfare began to give way to the politics of ideological dogma. This was fuelled by a growing public dissatisfaction with the level of service provided by the NHS in the 1970s. **Morgan, Calnal and Manning** (1985) point to how the bureaucratic legacy suffered by the NHS produced a service that was inconsistent and lacked continuity.

LABOUR REFORMS OF THE NHS (1974)

Political and public unhappiness with the quality of service provided by the NHS led to a major reform in 1974. The NHS was reorganised into a number of regional health authorities and district health authorities. The rationale underpinning this was that these changes would create a more efficient, centralised structure which would steward resources more effectively.

	Table 14: *Government spending on the NHS (1949–79)*	
YEAR	NHS EXPENDITURE AS A PERCENTAGE OF GNP	£M
1949	3.9	437
1959	3.8	792
1969	4.4	1733
1979	5.3	9082

SOURCE: ADAPTED FROM **TAYLOR AND FIELD** (1993)

The architects of the NHS wanted to create a health service that would provide for the needs of all. However, it was swamped by growing demands and rising expectations of what it could deliver. Costs spiralled and were added to by the needs of an ageing population (see Chapter 4) and the finance demanded by technological improvements. The pressure on the NHS took on the proportions of a crisis that shattered the postwar consensus for a free, universal health care upon which the NHS was founded.

The Labour Government of 1949–79 sought to solve the crisis by increasing taxation levels – thus apparently confirming the claims of the Conservatives that the Party had always been a 'tax and spend' party. However, in the Conservative Party a hybrid fusion of liberal free market thinking and conservative paternalism was moulding itself into a new political ideology: **the New Right**. As this position gained strength and gathered momentum, the Conservative Party rejected the idea of increasing taxation to pay for a bloated public sector that had become a bottomless pit. The Conservatives promised a radical programme of political change in their election manifesto and one of the main promises was a 'root and branch' reform of the health service.

Activity

Investigate the main features of the ideological divide that had grown between the two main political parties by the 1970s. Divide the class into two smaller groups representing the Labour Government of 1979 and the Conservative opposition. Debate this motion:

'The only way to provide for a modern, dependable health service is to increase taxes.'

THE CONSERVATIVE YEARS (1979–97)

Conservative Governments were able to dominate British politics for nearly 20 years during the 1980s and 1990s. Successive governments during this period moved away from collectivist notions about the welfare state and criticised the wasteful and inefficient nature of the service.

The 1979 administration was dominated by Margaret Thatcher's commitment to market liberalism. Values dedicated to economic freedom were accompanied by a sense that people needed clear guidance and control. The core values of this curiously mixed ideology were 'choice', 'opportunity' and 'responsibility'. Anti-statist, anti-welfarist views resulted in a hostility towards what were seen as inefficient state bureaucratic state bureaucratic machines which needed to be run on the lines of private industry.

The New Right announced a programme designed to 'roll back the frontiers of the State'. A key desire of this policy was to cut welfare costs and to make individuals more responsible for making their own health care provision.

Activity
Is a free and universal NHS possible in the UK?

Embedded into these Conservative reforms was the notion that the model provided by private enterprise was the best one to improve standards and increase efficiency. Privatisation of the state run monoliths – the NHS included – was to become a key feature of the radical changes of the 1980s. The NHS entered a period of change every bit as fundamental as that of 1948.

NEW RIGHT REFORMS

Essentially the Conservatives introduced a raft of policy reforms that took affect in three main areas:

- structural reforms
- management reforms
- private enterprise.

Structural reforms
The longevity of Conservative Government enabled the Party to introduce a number of changes that fundamentally altered the structure of the NHS. In 1982 the middle tier of the NHS was removed. The area health authorities were replaced by NHS trusts.

The Government was keen to introduce the principles of private enterprise to the health service and did so by establishing an internal market in health care. The original tiering system allowed funds to trickle down the various tiers within the NHS, from the regional health authorities to the district health authorities, to the hospitals. The internal market replaced this with the creation of two types of agency: **purchasers** and **producers**.

Purchasers (such as district health authorities, GP fundholders – doctors who had a budget to purchase specific services for patients registered with them) were allocated a budget to pay for the health care of a defined population.

Providers (such as hospitals, ambulance services and community health services) were to earn their money from the sale of their services. Providers were encouraged to adopt 'trust' status which allowed them to have various powers of self-management.

The rationale underpinning these changes was that competition would allow fundholders to shop around the hospital trusts for the best and most effective (or cheapest) treatment. As part of a contract, purchasers and providers would agree to the services to be provided, as well as the costs involved and the duration of the agreement.

One of the aims of this increased competition was to increase the funds being spent on primary care (GPS, district nurses etc) at the expense of the secondary sector (hospitals). The intention was to have more people treated at home or on an out-patient basis.

Activity
Can a health service be run on a system of private enterprise? Who would be the likely winners and losers in such an arrangement?

Management reforms

The Griffiths Report of 1983 advocated the introduction of general management principles to the NHS. This was more than an attempt to delineate managerial responsibilities: it was also designed to import various management techniques from the private sector in to the NHS, in order to cut costs and improve efficiency.

This new emphasis on managerialism encouraged a new breed of managers to enter the NHS. They came, primarily, from a business or self-employed background. They were schooled in the notions of maximising profit through the stewardship of resources. Supporters of this move argued that the NHS needed to become leaner and fitter, if it was to complete effectively with the private and voluntary sectors. The rise of the NHS manager had begun.

Private enterprise

The Conservatives were keen to introduce a 'self help' philosophy to encourage the care of the elderly, the sick and the mentally ill by family, friends and the wider community. This initiative became known as 'care in the community' and it was designed to take welfare clients out of institutional care and into the community.

In principle, the policy was an attractive one. It was widely seen to be more beneficial for sick and vulnerable people to be cared for in a familiar environment, as opposed to a cold and remote institution.

There would be an added financial bonus: it would be much cheaper compared to institutional care. In 1986, government officials estimated that it would cost

£100 a week to support the care of a frail, elderly person in their own home, compared to a cost of £295 per week for a bed in an NHS geriatric ward.

Opponents, however, suspected that the financial motive was the overriding concern driving this policy, rather than a genuine commitment to improving the care of vulnerable people within the community. The belief by critics that a gap between needs and resources would result seemed to be confirmed by a number of tragic cases in which recipients of the community care policy either harmed themselves or others, because they were left to their own devices.

CENTRALISATION AND HEALTH CARE – TARGETS AND QUOTAS

In general, the Conservative administrations of the 1980s actively pursued a policy of centralising control in many areas – local government, the Civil Service, education and health care. Power was transferred to the centre as the Government began taking a more authoritarian line with local health authorities, setting them detailed performance targets and establishing annual reviews.

In addition, the Government established a national standard for the NHS by introducing the **Patient's Charter** in 1992. It was argued that initiatives like this, and the publication of league tables would enable the public to understand the mission of the NHS and to check its performance levels.

An emphasis was placed on primary care and the employment contracts of GPs, dentists and pharmacists linked financial pay with performance for the first time.

POINTS OF EVALUATION

Not since 1948, has health care experienced such a period of radical, fundamental reform. The NHS, like many public institutions, was beset with a wave of reforms and changes that struck at the very core of the service. The changes have been met with a great deal of suspicion.

1 Opponents claim that the reforms are a 'Trojan horse', designed to start a process that will eventually lead to the wholesale privatisation of the NHS.
2 Critics accuse the purchaser–provider system of creating a two tiered service, advantaging those who can afford to pay. Even without resorting to private health care, some patients will receive better treatment if they are lucky enough to be registered with the new breed of 'wheeler dealer' fundholding GPs.
3 If health care is to be truly based on business principles, it is likely that some Trusts will go bankrupt if they cannot generate contracts. Will this mean that market forces will determine which people will have accessible health care?
4 A market-style NHS will resist expensive treatments.
5 Quantity will replace quality: the number of patients treated could become more important than how well they are treated.

6 Despite the arguments, it is maintained that these reforms were designed to cut costs and increase efficiency. However, there is no benchmark against which to measure this. The pre-reform NHS kept little information on costs. **McLachlan** (1990) has argued that the pre-1979 NHS provided a good quality service at a low cost.

7 The reforms led to a huge increase in administrative costs: the internal market alone cost about £750 million to set up.

IS AN NHS POSSIBLE?

The Conservative years introduced a new notion concerning the NHS: that free health care should only be made available to those who *cannot afford* to pay. The force of this argument was noted by **O'Donnell** (1992). Between 1979 and 1997 there was a shift in attitude in rightwing thinking that fundamentally rejected the principles that underpinned the formation of the NHS in 1948. Access to treatment would no longer be based solely on need, but would include the principle of rationing and, in some cases, the ability to pay.

Supporters of the reforms introduced in the period of Conservative rule argued that this was an inevitability. The rising expectations that people have of the health service, the ever increasing costs of advanced medical treatment and the financial drain placed upon the service by an ageing population created an ongoing crisis in health care.

The only way to deal with this is by some system of health rationing, New Right supporters argue. **Ham** (1992) agrees that this is a reality that any government will have to face. Indeed, those that can afford to pay for health care will have to. In this context, the New Right reforms have been seen as a pragmatic response to the problems created by supporting, in principle, a health care system that cannot be financed in practice.

Supporters of these changes argue that the reforms have led to more people being treated and lower costs in areas such as acute hospital care. Waiting times have been reduced and fundholding GPs have reported that they were able to purchase a more efficient service for their patients.

Clearly, there is now a major debate about the money allocated to health care in the UK and how that money is managed. It is this issue that currently engages the New Labour Government which was elected to power in 1997. It appears that we have now entered a period of **'welfare pluralism'** as anticipated by **Norman Johnson** (1987). From being the main provider of health care since 1948, has the State become one of only a variety of institutions dealing with health?

THE NHS SINCE 1997

As we write, it is too early to offer any real judgements on the record on the New Labour Government regarding health. The administration has made a number of promises and commitments that have yet to bear any real fruit.

New Labour have promised to end the internal market and have restated their commitment to the principle of a universal health care. A White Paper issued in December 1997 called **The New NHS – Modern, Dependable** provides an outline of the Government's intentions. Over the next decade the intentions are:

- to enhance primary care
- to decentralise responsibility for operational management
- to emphasise co-operation in order to create a partnership between local authorities, social service departments and voluntary organisations.

In 1998, a further White Paper was published entitled **Our Healthier Nation** which promised to take a more holistic view of health. It acknowledged the importance to health of factors such as housing, environment, education and lifestyle.

The aim appears to be *prevention rather than cure* and this will be achieved through a series of contracts involving government departments, health-related organisations, local authorities, voluntary organisations and charities, alongside bodies connected with education, housing and transport.

The contract will describe the role that each organisation can play in four priority areas:

1 heart disease and strokes
2 accidents
3 cancer
4 mental health.

The Government has signalled an intention to establish a co-ordinated programme that will include government and national players, local players, communities and individuals in a programme of health improvement.

At the local level, these should appear as health improvement programmes and they should be in place by April 1999. By the end of 1999, the Government intends to have established ten pilot **health action zones** in areas of great need.

The changes proposed by New Labour are still in their infancy, but they demonstrate how the debate about health care is subject to ongoing change. The debate over health remains at the cutting edge of the political agenda and students of this subject need an understanding of the historical context but, more importantly, an interest in contemporary developments.

SUMMARY

This chapter has traced in brief the developments that contributed to the creation of the NHS in 1948 and its development in the immediate postwar period, before focusing in more detail on the health policy issues that characterised the Conservative Party's terms of office between 1979 and 1997. We have attempted to demonstrate the importance of a sociological evaluation of the relationship between the organs of the State, the providers of health care and users of the service. In this context we will be able to evaluate the contemporary issues facing New Labour and the effectiveness of the proposed measures.

Group work

Your class has been invited to make a presentation to a visiting group of students from France on the current issues facing the NHS. Put together an oral presentation, complete with appropriate OHTs and handouts, on the following topic: 'The NHS – issues for the millennium'. Bear in mind the language skills of your audience and the context in which they will view the NHS. Some research into health care in France may be required.

Coursework

1 Conduct research to investigate the hypothesis that the original mission of the NHS to provide health care which is free at the point of delivery is now impossible to achieve.
2 Conduct an investigation into the provision of health care by carrying out a survey of people in your local area to discover if they are carers and what support they receive. Try to support this with some detailed case studies of the carers you discover.
3 Carry out research into NHS provision in your area by contacting local hospitals, Trusts, doctors and clinics. Establish how the NHS has changed in recent years from these perspectives. Carry out interviews with NHS clients to see how they perceive the service and the changes, and whether they feel that services have improved or declined.

Exam Hints

'Health care is more effectively provided by the private sector than the public sector.' Evaluate the sociological arguments for and against this point of view.

The private–public split in health care needs to be examined. It is a good idea to place this issue in an historical context. Begin by examining the provision of health care by the private sector before 1948 and assess whether it met the needs of the population. Continue by examining the performance of the NHS after 1950, critically examining the level of service that it provided. Examine the rationale behind the New Right reforms after 1979 and establish whether they produced a better health service by embracing the principles of private enterprise. Conclude by examining the implications of a health service largely run as a private sector arrangement, with a public service left to provide for those who cannot afford private treatment.

1 'The goal of the NHS has been to allocate health care resources equally among all groups of the population. It has failed in this mission.' Assess this view in the light of sociological arguments and evidence.

2 'The New Right reforms of the NHS were driven more by a need to cut costs than to improve the quality of health care in Britain.' Critically examine the Conservative reforms of the NHS in the light of this statement.

7

CONTEMPORARY DEBATES

Introduction

SO FAR IN this text we gave examined the contribution that sociology has made to an understanding of health care issues. We have explored the knowledge denied from and intellectual debates examined in the work of those who have developed this specialised branch of the discipline of sociology. **Stacey** (1998) argues that sociology has been responsible for more than just a theoretical, academic study of health, in that it has had a practical impact on the education and thinking of most health care professionals and medical practitioners.

This final chapter will examine the contemporary issues that are facing the health industry at the end of the twentieth century. These issues will probably set the agenda for sociological research in the twenty-first century. Some of the topics explored will be necessarily speculative and, in particular, it will not be possible to set out the definitive framework for the work of medical sociologists. Instead, the intention is to establish some signposts to indicate a number of possible directions that may be followed. By designating certain areas to be significant in the likely development of health, other matters of sociological importance in relation to health, illness and suffering may be overlooked. It is the intention of this chapter to suggest that areas not mentioned are not legitimate areas for sociological research. The challenge facing medical sociology is to be flexible enough to engage in research in the constantly changing agenda that health creates.

In looking to the future, it is also important to acknowledge the echoes of the past. Previous Chapters have explored the development of health care in the UK and have traced the rise of – and the challenges to – the bio-medical model of health. Chapter 3 noted how this model centres on a physiological view of health which defines health and ill health as objective, biological categories.

In recent years, this view has been subject to critical attention from many writers. The notion, implicit in the medical model – that illness has a causation, that it can be cured by medical science, that preventative measures are effective – has been challenged. The scepticism advanced by the social constructivist view has been accompanied by developments in alternative, complementary medicine. Indeed, it is interesting to theorise about whether the late twentieth century will witness a revival of a reinvented bio-medical model: one that is rooted in genetic arguments, that goes beyond a desire to find cures and focuses, instead, on engineering ill health out of people.

The study of health may enter new and uncharted waters. It is vital, therefore, that social scientists shadow these developments so that they can make a legitimate and valuable contribution.

Table 15: *Theorists, concepts and issues in this chapter*		
KEY THEORIST	KEY CONCEPTS	KEY ISSUES
Newell	Scientists will be able to make and shape genes	• Genetics will become the science of the twenty-first century
Nettleton	Body Fascism	• An intolerance of anyone who fails to live up to ideal notions of the body
Beck and Giddens	Risk society	• Reflexive modernity causes us all to adapt to a world of risky freedoms
Plummer	Medicine as surveillance	• AIDS has created technologies that have made incursions into people's lives

GENETIC ENGINEERING – PLAYING GOD?

Genetic engineering has been developing rapidly over the past 10 to 15 years. Simplistically it involves the movement of genes from one living organism to another and, at the moment, the most commonly used method imports genes into living cells that have been grown in laboratories. A future aim of the technique may be to manage the human body's internal chemistry – especially its ability to fight disease – in order to mimic the effect of drugs.

Another area of bioengineering, whilst still in its infancy, is potentially controversial. This is **gene therapy**. The aim is to treat people suffering from incurable diseases that are the result of genetic problems. Scientists hope to be able to replace the malfunctioning gene with a corrected version, thereby preventing or curing the disease.

A third strand of this research is much further advanced than human gene therapy and has already provoked considerable debate. This has focused on moving genes into plants in order to engineer better and disease-resistant crops. Moving genes from one species to another offers opportunities to improve performance of the whole plant. The technique may be used in the animal world in the future. Ideas already advanced in this field include the introduction of the genes from deep-sea fish into fruit to make them more resistant to frost. Opponents argue that this 'Frankenstein food' is an offence against nature. They cite the disastrous attempts by scientists to improve beef yield by feeding meat products to cattle in the 1980s and the resultant incidence of CJD, the human form of BSE or 'mad cow disease'.

A NEW BIO-MEDICAL MODEL

These developments are important sociologically as well as medically. Potentially, we are witnessing the birth of a renewed version of the bio-medical view of health. This model may go beyond the traditional view that considers illness as necessitating either prevention or cure. The new model could view illness, disease, abnormality, disability and, perhaps even death, as 'problems' that could be engineered through genetic technology.

Genetic engineering and the implications for human life

In 1988, a body was set up to co-ordinate the various strands of research that were being carried out on human genome research. It is called HUGO: the Human Genome Organisation. The brief of this organisation is to avoid the duplication of human genome research and to attempt to co-ordinate the work of scientists working in this field of research. There are currently about 2000 scientists working on this project and their aim is to specify the exact sequences of the (approximately) 3000 million pairs of bases in all the DNA in a typical human cell.

Theoretically, if the DNA sequence can be established, researchers will be able to work towards bio-engineered genes to prevent or cure conditions like cancer and heart disease. HUGO is anticipated to wind down somewhere around 2005. Already it has put forward a number of amazing advanced pronouncements:

- There will be new treatments for cardio vascular disease and cancer.
- Humans will have an unlimited supply of replacement organs cloned from their own cells, thereby removing the risk of rejection in transplant surgery.
- The genes that control ageing will be identified, allowing the process to be decelerated.

Genetic engineering has already set out to create vaccines for major tropical diseases such as malaria and bilharzia (sleeping sickness). Bioengineers are developing parasite genes to create antigens which will stimulate human immunity. Having isolated parasite genes which code for antigens, they can be cloned in laboratory cultures. Bacteria can be made to express the parasite antigens which can be collected, purified and turned into vaccines. Success in the field of tropical medicines has led to scientists turning their attention to diseases such as polio, typhoid and smallpox.

There is hope within the scientific community that these principles can be extended to combat other virally transmitted diseases, such as cervical cancer and AIDS. In addition, the identification of oncogenes (genes, which, when defective, encourage cancerous cell growth) and anti-oncogenes (tumour suppressants that can prevent cell growth) have created possibilities for the genetic treatment of cancer.

Study point

Prepare an oral report for your class on bioengineering. Discuss the new treatments that it may offer for diseases in the next few years. Are the treatments 'better' than current therapies?

THE ETHICS OF BIOENGINEERING

Bioengineering is more than a medical issue. Clearly, there are deep ethical and moral questions, in addition to the philosophical and practical concerns.

Activity

Is there a danger that scientists are beginning to 'play God'? Discuss the ethical and moral issues raised by the prospect of genetic engineering. Add these arguments to your oral presentation.

Implicit in the idea of using genes in treatments is the concept of normality in human health. Is it desirable that one gene should be seen as normal and another as abnormal? What does this say about the people carrying the genes?

Advances in genetic engineering create two possibilities:

1 *Somatic* – scientists can intervene to prevent malformation.
2 *Positive* – Scientists can engineer genes to make us healthier.

Could we breed out the malformed, the disabled, the imperfect? If so, where would the line be drawn? In the past, eugenics programmes have been considered completely unethical. Where will we stand in the future?

As well as this notion of normality, sociologists will need to consider many related factors such as the likely impact of a much longer human lifespan. In pre-industrial times and shortness of people's lives facilitated early marriage. Relationships survived the short duration of the partners' lives. As we have seen in Chapter 4, health advances have lengthened the human lifespan considerably this century, and not without cost. As people now realistically expect to live long lives, marriages and long term relationships have been delayed. The biological deadlines on mating have been systematically moved back. Many relationships founder and fail because the individuals involved find it difficult to sustain a deep emotional commitment over an ever increasing length of time.

Chapter 6 considered the demographic changes that have resulted in more and more people living into their 80s. Sociologically, we need to consider the massive social consequences that would result from people living even longer. Human relationships will probably change still further. Given that, with medical intervention, women can now conceive children after the menopause this raises the distinct possibility that people will have the time to raise two, or even three, entirely different families. People will have vastly different experiences in a whole range of social areas.

Activity
Consider the implications of a society in which people could live to 130. What changes could result in marriage, education, work and leisure?

THE SOCIOLOGY OF THE BODY

Turner (1989) argues that we are progressively moving towards a **somatic society** in which the body has become a central focus of political and cultural activity. This is an idea supported **Nettleton** (1995) who argues that social changes have fundamentally altered the way in which we view our bodies. We are now much more aware of our bodies than ever before.

Indeed, as the boundary between the physical body and society has become increasingly blurred, the sociology of the body represents an important and fruitful area of study. Medical and technological advances have raised important moral, ethical, medical and religious questions about issues such as abortion, reproduction and euthanasia. Moreover, the issues raised by an ageing population mean that sociology and medicine have to consider the nature of ageing and death, and to confront the social taboos surrounding these issues. Euthanasia is significant here as it could be regarded by some as a viable alternative to employing new treatments for diseases and to caring for older people.

DR DAVID MOORE INVOLVED IN UP TO 50 CASES OF EUTHANASIA ARRIVING AT THE WEST END POLICE STATION, NEWCASTLE IN NOVEMBER 1997 TO FIND OUT IF ANY CHARGES WILL BE BROUGHT AGAINST HIM. EUTHANASIA WILL BECOME AN INCREASINGLY DEBATED ISSUE DURING THE TWENTY-FIRST CENTURY.

THE MEDIA AND THE BODY

It is important to consider the role that the media plays in the elevation of the body. Many observers claim that society has entered a post-modern period in which the image has become reality. An esoteric, avant garde philosophy has developed in the last 10 years that has challenged sociology's ability – and indeed the ability of any human discipline – to provide coherent explanations about the modern world. Ironically, by claiming that it is impossible to provide a grand explanation, or **meta-narrative**, about anything post modernists are, themselves, putting forward a rather grand theory.

Many post-modern thinkers focus in the powerful influence that the media has upon shaping our 'realty'. **Baudrillard** (1993a) argues that, for many people, actual reality and media reality have become virtually indistinguishable. Individuals take for granted knowledge that they consider to be 'real', whereas this is knowledge created by an entirely simulated or reproduced world. People know more about fictional neighbours than their real ones and what they 'know' is largely what they have learnt from the media. Baudrillard calls this the hyper-real and it is a development of the notion explored by Eco (1987), who sees this as being 'more real than real'.

Featherstone (1991a) argues that media images about the body have led to a 'cult of the body', in which an ideal notion about the body and health is packaged and sold to people as another consumer item. Interestingly, another 'ism' is implied here – **bodyism**. Nettleton refers to a 'body and health fascism' that is intolerant of those who fail to live up to the body norm: people with a disability or chronic illness, or merely those who are overweight.

Activity

Carry out your own research into the main features of post-modern analysis. Start with the work of Foucault to see how these ideas can be applied to health.

REFLEXIVITY AND THE BODY

Beck and Giddens are particularly scathing about post-modernism's rejection of grand narratives and general theory. For them, the present and the near future demands something like a 'second Enlightenment'; a period of more reason, not less, an epoch of self-criticism, humanity and reflexivity. Giddens (1991) examines the impact of modernity upon the self. He views the self in the world as a reflexive project. Essentially, this means that, as individuals, we reflect increasingly upon ourselves and our place in the world. In this process we create, maintain and recreate ourselves. This is a project driving all individuals in the modern world. Our concern with image manifests itself in a preoccupation with diet, exercise and health that is no longer proscribed by tradition or anchored in social conventions. In a 'pick and mix' society we are surrounded by a plethora of books, magazines, television programmes and videos that offer all manner of advice about lifestyle choices, fitness and health. Indeed, in an increasingly secular world, the loss of faith in an after life may have resulted in more people desperately attempting to prolong their existing lives. Health, diet and fitness thus become mechanisms for living longer.

Beck (1992a) is critical of the notion that we have entered an era of post-modernity. Rather, we have entered a period of 'radicalised' or reflexive modernity; a 'risk society' in which health and health-related issues become a way of coping with a world of risky freedoms.

THE BODY AND IDENTITY

The body has become a legitimate area of concern for sociology. The concept of the body can be seen as something that is socially constructed and manipulated. **Susie Orbach** (1993) argues that anorexia (starving oneself) and bulimia (bingeing and vomiting) are primarily female problems created by a desire to conform to the ideological image of the body. Feminists, such as **Dutton** (1995), argues that women have spent centuries responding to male manipulation of their bodies.

Giddens offers us the notion of personal meaningless in modern life. As we continually avoid confronting serious issues such as sickness and death and treat them as taboos, we will be driven to find meaning in projects designed to make us healthy and beautiful.

Activity

Collect a series of teenage, women's and men's magazines. Analyse them to see if they project images of strength, vulnerability, slimness etc. Can Gidden's ideas about reflexivity and self-identify be applied to these magazines?

Leder (1992) suggests that we take our bodies largely for granted until they malfunction and **Shilling** (1993) puts forward the notion that the body is an unfinished biological and social entity which is developed by social expectations. In a risk society, our bodies are subject to a social control that is imposed upon us from four main spheres: the personal, religion, medicine and law.

Activity

Consider ways in which individuals and social groups exercise control over the body in the four categories suggested by Shilling.

A great deal of the research on the sociology of the body has been inspired by the work of Foucault, who argued that medicine has controlled the body and has exercised surveillance over it. **Turner** (1987) instructs us to see the body as both biologically and socially constructed. This echoed the work of **Elias**, (1978) who traced how, from the Middle Ages onwards, the body has been subject to increasing regulation by medicine. Its functions are viewed as shameful and dirty by individuals and social groups.

The sociology of the body is, therefore, at the leading edge of a lot of academic sociological study. It represents a forum which allows us to discuss a variety of issues, such as the stigma that is attached to disability and that often leads to those with disabilities being stereotyped and de-sexed. We can also consider whether it has contributed to a hardening of attitudes towards the chronically ill. Nettleton describes how the chronically sick are expected to conform to a particular social view – that, if they are not expected to improve, they should not be too demanding. They have already challenged what Talcott Parsons identified as the 'sick role' in the 1950s. This is a role in which we allow people a temporary escape from normal expectations of they are ill, but only if they seek to get better.

In addition, this branch of sociology allows us to explore the sociological importance of death, dying and bereavement. Indeed, the treatment of the terminally ill in our society is a crucial one for health policy, spilling into areas such as palliative care for the elderly, euthanasia and the 'right to die' for individuals who have terminal or untreatable illnesses.

We have already seen how Giddens believes that the taboos surrounding death and dying have resulted in people who are unable to speak about these in a demedicalized context. The issues surrounding death, dying and bereavement are massively important. However, in an age that sees these are much more avoidable than before, relatively few young people experience the personal trauma of death. Death seems to be confined to specific social groups such as the old. Elderly people expect to lose family and friends, and we expect to lose them. Deaths of younger people from AIDS have been primarily confined to 'risk' groups such as homosexuals, drug addicts and the sexually promiscuous. This may also allow us to distance ourselves from death, if the context does not apply to us.

THE CHALLENGE OF AIDS

In fact, the AIDS experience has led to a re-examination of health and illness in a number of ways. It acts as a potent reminder that medicine cannot cure every ill and that there are limits to medical technology and medical expertise. It has prompted scientists to search for a cure, in order to restore faith in the principles implicit in the bio-medical model.

Genetic engineering has encouraged us to believe that medicine and science are only temporarily stalled by AIDS in the march of progress towards a cure for all diseases. Several different paths are being followed to try and create effective vaccines for the disease. Proponents of genetic engineering maintain that, without bioengineering, there would have been no way of establishing how HIV infects cells, let alone consider ways of defeating it. Current research is focusing on how the virus enters the body through the T-cells and infects them via a receptor known as CD4. The goal is to clone and express a gene for CD4 in the laboratory. Then it may be possible to manufacture receptor material to bolster the human immune system.

HIV and AIDS has left a wake of tragedy and death. The World Health Organisation predicts that by the year 2000, there will be 30 million HIV-infected adults and 10 million children infected worldwide. In cities such as New York, Aids has become the leading cause of death of women in the 20–40 age category according to **Holmes** (1993).

The appalling spread of the disease raises a number of crucial sociological questions. **Weeks** (1989) traces how, throughout its short history, AIDS has been simultaneously medicalized as 'diseased' and moralised as 'stigma', This can be traced through a history of the disease, which has gone from an awareness of the crisis in the early 1980s, to a moral panic in the middle of the decade, to an attempt to manage the crisis from 1985 until the present. This brief history flags up a number of important issues relating to the role of doctors and practitioners. The disease was unique in that it represented a combination of sex, drugs, death and infection. The idea that it represented some form of 'gay plague' meant that for several years research and health intervention was delayed. The contagion seemed to be confined to marginal groups who were both politically and morally 'embarrassing'. The moral panic and New Right moral majority views in America forced some health care practitioners to adopt a stance against the 'guilt' HIV/AIDS sufferers (homosexuals, bisexuals, injecting drugs users) in favour of the 'innocent' carriers (haemophiliacs, babies born infected). This trend was resisted by the British medical profession, but it serves to illustrate the point that medicine does not exist in a social and political vacuum.

Prevention or surveillance?

AIDS has a high mortality rate and, as yet, no known cure. Preventative measures have been advanced with education as the most important tool. HIV education has encouraged monogamy and 'safe sex' using condoms. For some sociologists, this is more than just a question of health education, it is also another medical incursion into people's lives. **Plummer** (1988) expresses a concern that the disease has provided a further opportunity for the medical profession to monitor the activities of people:

With the symbolism of AIDS has emerged a range of institutional practices that aim to increase surveillance and regulation over "deviances" and "sexualities", many new agencies have appeared along with many new practices that aim to keep records, classify and order, take tests, watch over, maybe brand and quarantine people on the AIDS spectrum.

Here there are shades of Foucault – medicine acting as a form of knowledge in which different notions of health and illness affect the way people understand, explain and talk about health. Foucault calls this the 'discourse' of medicine, in which knowledge is related to power. Health and illness, therefore, depend on who has the ability to define the state that our body is in.

As we have seen, medicine acting in a surveillance capacity is nothing new. In the nineteenth century, medical practice emerged from the need to supervise the large populations that were growing in the new towns and cities. The weakening of the hold of the bio-medical model in the late twentieth century has seen the onus for good health transferred to individuals, who should take responsibility for their own health. In this context, the role of doctors has increasingly shifted to one of surveillance. Medical practitioners monitor and supervise, offering rational advice on how to avoid ill health. This has also made individuals culpable in their health – much illness can be viewed as a result of wilful self-harm. Sociology is invited to explore ideas about who controls the body and the power that is wielded by institutions such as the medical profession and the media.

In conclusion, the study of AIDS offers sociology a number of strands of enquiry:

- sexual behaviours
- gender differences in sexual behaviours
- the role of education
- the role of genetic engineering
- the question about medical surveillance and control.

SUMMARY

It is difficult to anticipate what will be the crucial issues facing sociology in the next century. It is possible that genetic engineering, the sociology of the body and the impact of AIDS will be high on the agenda for sociological health-policy research in the next century and that these areas are ones in which sociology can continue to play a key role.

STUDY ⬢ GUIDES

Group work

Discuss the impact of medical developments alongside environmental progress in improving the health of those in an industrial society like Britain's.

Coursework

1 Investigate the hypothesis that 'our preoccupation with health and fitness is part of a reflexive project that involves us all'.
2 Investigate the notion that the body is an unfinished biological and social entity that is awaiting the expectations of society.

Exam Hints

'Society gives doctors the power to label a person sick.' Discuss the implications of this statement for an understanding of the nature of ill-health.

This essay requires you to discuss the bio-medical model of ill-health and the power that has been assumed by doctors as a result. There will also be an opportunity to consider the power of health practitioners to label the sick and the ill. You will need to examine the concept of the 'sick role', as well as the work of Goffman and Foucault who have both examined the power of medicine to define and label illness. Try to balance your answer by considering the genuine attempt by doctors to heal, as well as control, and consider the contributions that have been made to this argument by the social constructivists.

Practice Questions

1 'Doctors have a monopoly power over health care and exercise this largely in their own interest.' Critically consider this statement.
2 Critically examine the view that the body and illness are nothing more than the discourses used to describe them.
3 Critically consider the moral and ethical dilemmas that are raised by the new directions taken by generic research.

SELECTED REFERENCES

BIBLIOGRAPHY

Bartley, M. et al (1996) 'Measuring Inequalities in Health: an Analysis of Mortality Patterns Using Two Social Classifications', *Sociology of Health and Illness*, Vol 18, No 4.

Baudrillard, J. (1993a) *Simulations*, New York, Semiotext(e).

Beck, U. (1992) *Risk Society: Towards a New Modernity*, London, Sage.

Beck, U. (1997) *The Re-invention of Politics*, Cambridge, Polity Press.

Beck, U., Giddens, A. and Lash, S. (1994) *Reflexive Modernisation*, Cambridge, Polity Press.

Berger, P. and Luckmann, T. (1966) *The Social Construction of Reality*, Penguin.

Bury, M.R. (1987) 'Social Constructionism and Medical Sociology', *Sociology of Health and Illness*, Vol. 9.

Cartwright, A. and O'Brien, M. (1976) 'Social Class Variations in Health Care and in General Practitioner Consultations', The Sociology of the NHS, *Sociology Review*, Monograph 22, University of Keele.

Crawford, M. (1977) 'You are dangerous to your health', *Inernational Journal of Health Services*, Vol 7, No 7.

Croall, H. (1992) *White Collar Crime*, OUP.

Croall, H. (1993) 'White Collar Crime', *Sociology Review*, Vol 3, No. 2.

Culley, L. and Dyson, S. (1993) 'Race, Inequality and Health', *Sociology Review*, Vol 3, No 1.

Doyal, L. (1995) *What Makes Women Sick? Gender and the Political Economy of Health*, Basingstoke, MacMillan.

Dutton, K.R. (1995) *The Perfectible Body: the Western Idea of Physical Development*, London, Cassell.

Eco, U. (1987) *Travels in Hyper-reality*, London, Picador.

Elias, N. (1978) *The Civilising Process*, Oxford, Blackwell (orig. pub. 1939).

Epstein, H. (1998) 'Relative Deprivation and Life Expectancy', *S-Sociology Magazine*, September, Issue 1.

Featherstone, M. (1991a), *Consumer Culture in Post-Modernism*, London, Sage.

Ferrie, J.E. et al (1995) 'Health Effects of Anticipation of Job Change and Non-Employment: Longitudinal Data from the Whitehall II Study', *BMJ*

Foucault, M. (1983) 'Social Security', reproduced in Kritzman, L.K. (ed) *Politics, Philosophy and Culture* (trans. Sheridan, A.) New York, Routledge.

Foucault, M. (1963) *The Birth of the Clinic: an Archaeology of Medical Perception*, New York, Routledge.

Fox, N.J. (1993) *Postmodernism, Sociology and Health*, Oxford, OUP.

Friedson, S. (1992) *The Handbook of Complementary Medicine*, Oxford, OUP.

Fulder, S. (1992) *The Handbook of Complementary Medicine*, Oxford, OUP.

Giddens, A. (1991) *Modernity and Self-Identity*, Cambridge, Polity Press.

Goffman, E. (1961, 1968) *Asylums: Essays on the Social Situation of Mental Patients and Other Inmates*, Harmondsworth: Penguin.

Goffman, E. (1970) *Stigma: Notes on the Management of Spiritual Identities*, Harmondsworth: Penguin.

Graham, H. and Oakley, A. (1981) 'Competing Ideologies of Reproduction: Medical and Maternal Perspectives on Pregnancy', in Roberts, H. (ed) *Women, Health and Reproduction*, London, Routledge.

Graham, H. (1989) *Health and Welfare*, Basingstoke, Macmillan.

Graham, H. (1992) *Issues of Sociology: Health and Welfare*, London, Nelson.

Holmes, K. (1993) 'The Changing Epidemiology of HIV Transmission', in Corey, L. *Aids: Problems and Perspectives*, London, Norton Medical Books.

Holmes, T.H. and Rahe, R.H. (1967) 'The Social Readjustment Rating Scale', *Journal of Psychomatic Research* II.

Hugo (1988) *The Human Genome Organisation*.

Hum (1992) *Health Policy in Britain*, 3rd ed, Basingstoke, MacMillan.

Hunt, S. and Lightly, N. (1999) 'A Health Alternative? A Sociology of Fringe Medicine', *Sociology Review*, Vol 8, No. 3.

Illich, I. (1976) *Medical Nemesis: Limits to Medicine*, London, Boyars.

Illich, I. (1990) *Limits to Medicine: Medical Nemesis: the Expropriation of Health*, Harmondsworth, Penguin.

Johnson, N. (1987) *The Welfare State in Transition*, Brighton, Wheatsheaf.

Krimskey, S. (1992) 'The Role of Theory in Risk Studies' in Krimskey, S. and Golding, D. (eds) *Social Theories of Risk*, Connecticut, Preger.

Leder, D. (ed) (1992) *The Body Medical Thought and Practice*, London, Kluwer Academic.

Lehr (?) *Stereotyping of Age and Age Norms*.

Lement, E. (1967) *Human Deviance, Social Problems and Social Control*, Englewood Cliff NJ, Prentice Hall.

Lyotard, J-F. (1984) *The Postmodern Condition: A Report on Knowledge*, Manchester, Maidert UP.

Lyotard, J-F. (1992) 'Abandoning the Metanarratives of Modernity', in Hall, S. et al (ed) *Modernity and its Futures*, Polity, Cambridge.

Mares, P, Larbie, J. and Baxter, C. (1987) *Training in Multi-Racial Health Care*, Cambridge, National Extension College.

Martin, E. (1989) *The Woman in the Body: A Cultural Analysis of Reproduction*, Buckingham, OUP.

McKeown, T. (1976) *The Role of Medicine, Dream, Mirage or Nemesis?*, Oxford, Basil Blackwell.

McKeown, T. (1979) *The Role of Medicine*, Oxford, Blackwell.

McNaught, A. (1987) *Race and Health Policy*, Croomhelm.

Medical Research Council (1994) *The Health of the UK's Elderly People*.

Midwinter, E. (1984) *The Development of Social Welfare in Britain*, Buckingham, OUP.

Morgan, M., Culnal, M. and Manning, M. (1985) *Sociological Approaches to Health and Medicine*, London, Routledge.

Navarro, V. (1976) *Medicine under Capitalism*, London, Crromhelm.

Navarro, V. (1978) *Class Struggle, The State and Medicine*, London, Martin Robinson.

Nettleton, S. (1995) *The Sociology of Health and Illness*, Cambridge, Polity Press.

Nettleton, S. (1996) 'Women and the New Paradigm of Health and Medicine', *Critical Social Policy*, Vol 24, London, Sage.

Newell, J. (1991) *Playing God: Engineering with Genes*, London, Broadside Books.

O'Donnell, M. (1992) 'Your Good Health', *Sociology Review*, Vol 2, No 1.

Oakley, A. (1984) *The Captured Womb*, Oxford, Blackwell.

Orbach, S. (1993) *Hunger Strike: The Anoretic's Struggle as a Metaphor of our Age*, Harmondsworth, Penguin.

Parons, T. (1951) *The Social System*, New York, Free Press.

Pfeffer, N. (1987) 'Artificial insemination, in vitro fertilisation and the stigma of infertility', in Stanworth, M. (ed) *Reproductive Technologies; Gender, Motherhood and Medicine*, Cambridge, Polity Press.

Plummer, K. (1988) 'Organising AIDS', in Aggleton, P. and Homans, H. (eds) *Social Aspects of AIDS*, London, Falmer Press.

Porter, R. (1986) *Patients and Practitioners: Lay Perceptions of Medicine in Pre-Industrial Society*, Cambridge: CUP.

Porter, M. (1990) 'Professional-Client Relationships and Women's Reproductive Health Care', in Cunningham-Burley, S. and McKeganey, N. (ed) *Readings in Medical Sociology*, London, Tavistock Routledge.

Rogers, W.S. (1991) *Explaining Health and Illness*, Hemel Hempstead, Harvester/Wheatsheaf.

Rosenhan, DL. (1975) 'On being sane in insane places', *Journal of Abnormal Psychology*, 84(5).

Scambler, G. (ed) (1991) *Sociology as Applied to Medicine*, 3rd ed, Balliere Tindall.

Scott, R. (1969) *The Making of Blind Men: A Study in Adult Socialisation*, in *Sociology Review*, Vol 4, No. 1.

Scull, A. (1984) *Decaceration: Community Treatment and the Deviant: A Radical View*, London, Polity Press.

Sedgwick, P. (1972) 'Mental Illness is Illness', paper presented to the *National Deviancy Conference*, 10th Deviency Symposium, York.

Senior, M. (1993) 'Health, Illness and Postmodernism', *Sociology Review*, Vol 6, No 1.

Senior, H. (1996) 'Health, Illness and Postmodernism', *Sociology Review*, Vol 6, No 1.

Sharma, U. (1992) *Complementary Medicine Today*, London, Routledge.

Sheeran, Y. (1995) 'Sociology, Biology and Health', *Sociology Review*, Vol 4, No. 4.

Shilling, C. (1993) *The Body and Social Theory*, London, Sage.

Smith, Bartley and Blane (1990) 'The Black Report on Socio-Economic

Inequalities in Health – Ten Years On' *BMJ*, Vol 3, No 1.

Stacey, M. (1998) *The Sociology of Health and Healing*, London, Unwin Hyman.

Stainton Rogers, W. (1991) *Explaining Health and Illness: an Explanation of Diversity*, Hemel Hempstead, Harvester/Wheatsheaf.

Szasz, T.S. (1974) *The Myth of Mental Illness*, New York, Harper and Row.

Taylor, S. and Field, D. (eds) (1993) *Sociology of Health and Health Care*, Oxford, Blackwell Science.

Townshend, P. and Davidson, N. (1992) *Inequalities in Health*, London, Penguin.

Trowler, P. (1989) *Investigating Health, Welfare and Poverty*, London, Unwin Hyman.

Trower, P. (1996) *Investigating Health, Welfare and Poverty*, London, Collins Educational.

Tudor-Hart, J. (1971) 'The Inverse Care Law' *The Lancet* 27.02.71.

Turner, B.S. (1987) *Medical Power and Social Knowledge*, London, Sage.

Turner, B.S. (1989) *The Body and Society*, Oxford, Basil Blackwell.

Twaddle, A.C. (1973) 'Illness and Deviance', *Social Science and Medicine*, Vol 7.

Wadsworth, M. (1986) 'Serious Illness in Childhood and its association with Later Life Achievement'

Weeks, J. (1989) 'AIDS: the intellectual agenda', in Aggleton, P., Hart, G. and Davies, P (ed) *AIDS: Social Representations, Social Practices*, London, Falmer Press.

Wells, C. (1993) *Corporations and Criminal Responsibility*, Oxford, OUP.

Whitehead, M. (1987) *The Health Divide*, Health Education Council.

Widgery, D. (1979) *Health in Danger: the Crisis in the NHS*, London, Papermac.

Wiles, R. and Higgins, J. (1996) *Health and Illness*, Vol 18, No 3.

Wilkinson, R. (1997) *Unhealthy Society: the Afflictions of Inequality*, London, Routledge.

Wilkinson, R. (1998) 'Unhealth Society: How Inequality Kills', *Sociology Review*, Vol 7, No 4.

Wilkinson, R.G. (1986a) *Class and Health: Research and Longitudinal Data*, London, Tavistock.

Witz, A. (1992) *Professions and Patriarchy*, London, Routledge.

World Health Organisation (1984) 'Health Promotion: a Discussion Document on the Concept and Principles' Copenhagen: Regional Office for Europe.

World Health Organisation (1986) 'Ottawa Charter for Health Promotion: Ottowa Health and Welfare', Canadian Public Health Association.

HEALTH PUBLICATIONS

Health Education Authority published by The Health Educational Authority, Marston Books Services, PO Box 269, Abingdon, Oxon, OX14 4TN.

Health in England published by The Office for National Statistics and the Health Education Authority, HMSO, PO Box 276, London SW8 5DT.

The NHS Handbook published by The NHS Confederation and JMH Publishing, 7 Stafford Road, Conford Lane, Tunbridge Wells, Kent TN2 4QZ.

WEBSITES

www.achoo.com/	*Healthcare Directory*
www.disabilitynet.co.uk	*Disability Net*
www.hea.org.uk	*General Health Information*
www.hsj.macmillan.com	*Health Services Journal*
www.interact.hea.liv.ac.uk	*Multimedia and Healthy Living*
www.nhs50.uk	*Fiftieth Anniversary site of the NHS*
www.niss.ac.uk/subject/61menu.html	*Focal Point for Information Resources Worldwide*
www.ohsu.edu/cliiweb	*Access to Clinical Information on the Web*
www.open.gov.uk	*Look for Department of Health's home page*
(www.open.gov.uk/doh/dhhome.htm)	
www.who.ch/	*World Health Organisation*

INDEX